ARE THOSE REAL?

TRUE TALES OF PLASTIC SURGERY FROM BEVERLY HILLS

NORMAN LEAF, MD

iUniverse, Inc.
New York   Bloomington

iUniverse books may be ordered through booksellers or by contacting:

iUniverse
1663 Liberty Drive
Bloomington, IN 47403
www.iuniverse.com
1-800-Authors (1-800-288-4677)

Because of the dynamic nature of the Internet, any Web addresses or links contained in this book may have changed since publication and may no longer be valid. The views expressed in this work are solely those of the author and do not necessarily reflect the views of the publisher, and the publisher hereby disclaims any responsibility for them.

ISBN: 978-1-4502-1840-5 (sc)
ISBN: 978-1-4502-18429- (dj)
ISBN: 978-1-4502-1841-2 (ebook)

Library of Congress Control Number: 2010903718

Printed in the United States of America

iUniverse rev. date: 04/12/2010

DEDICATION

For my mentors:

> Dr. Hilger Perry Jenkins, who showed me that a surgeon can be
> kind and gentle;
> Dr. Robert Chase, who opened my eyes to the wonder of plastic
> surgery;
> Dr. Harvey Zarem, who taught me the skills;
> Dr. Michael Gurdin, who taught me the art.

And for my wife, Judy Brand Leaf, who taught me to recognize
baloney when I see it, especially in myself.

CONTENTS

INTRODUCTION

The blink of an eye: more than thirty years have flashed by since I began practicing plastic surgery in Beverly Hills. The specialty and the city have both changed dramatically. Plastic surgery is no longer a subject cloaked in secrecy, reserved for the rich and famous. It's a media-packaged talisman of affluence—out there on the street, in your face, and in your living room. The city itself has evolved from a small town, albeit one with wealthy, famous residents, to a larger-than-life Mecca where medicine, glamour, and star power converge. There are other deservedly well-regarded centers of plastic surgery, but only Beverly Hills is looked to as the *focal point* of the specialty, the place where all the Famous Ones go for their lifts, tucks, and enhancements.

This isn't just hype or illusion. It's true—or at least mostly true—and the stars are closely followed by the stargazers, the spin doctors, and a multitude of believers eager to appear younger, thinner, bigger (breasted), and sexier than any reasonable person would care to be. A reality-based concept of plastic surgery has been displaced by a mass of exaggeration and gossip, eagerly fueled by a sensationalist media, and this concept has spread worldwide like a computer virus. Somewhere along the way, the disparity between fantasy and reality has blurred.

One point of clarification: this book is mostly about the *cosmetic*

1

aspects of plastic surgery. There is more to the specialty than simply making people look prettier; *reconstructive plastic surgery* deals with anything involving restoration of the normal human form and function. Many of our patients have severe deformities resulting from civilian or military trauma. Others require reconstruction after mastectomy or resection of head and neck cancer. Still others have the misfortune to be born with congenital anomalies of the face, body, or extremities. All board-certified plastic surgeons have extensive training in those types of procedures, too.

Another clarification: many presume that the specialty has something to do with *plastics*. In fact, plastic materials are often utilized, as in breast implants, for example. But the term really comes from the Greek word *plastikos,* which refers to shape, form, or structure.

I've written this book for several reasons. It's a short book, hopefully an interesting read, and it's definitely *not* intended to be an unbiased compendium of everything dished up on the menu of plastic surgery. There are lots of other books that provide that, along with an infinite number of Google-able Web sites. Rather, it is a *highly biased* personal view of the subject from the vantage point of one doctor (me) with over thirty years of experience in the trenches of Beverly Hills's Platinum Triangle. It will help debunk mythology and clear up misperceptions. It will show that even when seen stripped of all pretense and media razzle-dazzle, plastic surgery is still pretty exciting and marvelous. It will present a reasonably accurate portrait of the state of the art as it is practiced today in the fabled, fishbowl microcosm of Beverly Hills. And by means of some personal experiences I've had with my patients, I'll illustrate the good, the bad, the happy, the sad, and the just plain funny aspects of plastic surgery.

How does an Oscar winner feel about having a face-lift? What does a sexy leading lady do if her implants become hard and obvious?

What does an aging leading man think when he has a love scene with an actress half his age? How many days before a red-carpet event can one get eyelid surgery so that it heals and isn't picked up on today's high-definition TV cameras? Why do intelligent people who should know better get bad "plastic-looking" results? There are a thousand questions that you have perhaps never even thought to ask, or if you did, you probably didn't know whom to ask.

Plastic surgery is not a subject devoid of a human face or breast or abdomen. It is a powerful discipline that alters and usually improves the lives of people with many different backgrounds, not just movie stars. Some famous celebrities will be mentioned here, but their identities will be deliberately and definitively obscured. I have been lucky to have met and worked with some of the most famous, talented, and interesting people in the world, along with many, many more who no one outside their immediate families and friends will ever know. They each have a story, and a few of those stories are related in this volume.

Despite the extremes that the media uses to describe plastic surgery, most patients, even those in the uniquely fabled city of Beverly Hills, do not want to end up looking like their favorite celebrity or reinvent themselves with a complete makeover. They don't always want to look younger, and they especially don't want to look "altered." They simply want some help in achieving the confidence that comes from becoming the best possible, most attractive version of themselves. Those having dreams of magical transformation are warned that they might have a sad and expensive awakening.

For those interested in the *reality* (a seriously overworked word these days) of plastic surgery, please read on. Even without the extremes, the routinely achieved realities rival fiction for their impact and drama, and they are readily available at your neighborhood surgicenter or hospital—even if your zip code isn't 90210.

CHAPTER ONE
THE ROAD TO HOLLYWOOD

❖ *How I Got Here*

A screen memory: I was about nine years old when my father brought home our first television, a round-screen black-and-white Philco. We lived in a modest apartment on the south side of Chicago, and my parents felt that the best place to put the TV set was in the corner of the dining room rather than a coveted site in the living room near the plastic slipcovered sofa. By default, my favorite place to watch television became the cozy space beneath the dining room table. I would lie on my stomach with my hands supporting my head, my legs outstretched around the central table legs that were designed to pull apart if the table was lengthened for large dinner parties. In this position, I watched my favorite shows: *Captain Video, Garfield Goose, Howdy Doody,* and *Kukla, Fran and Ollie.* And there was one other iconic image that became permanently embedded in my consciousness.

One day each year, my attention was riveted on a real-world event. On New Year's Day, while there was frozen, dirty snow piled up over the curbs and the frost on the windows was too thick to see through, the Rose Parade was broadcast from Pasadena directly into my heart.

There was sunshine, mountains, flowers, beautiful blond girls, and convertibles. For a young boy accustomed to the frequently grim, confining cityscape of Chicago, the lure of California was irresistible. Somehow I knew that when I grew up, I would move to California, buy a convertible, and marry a blond.

It was that simple.

Around that time, I began to inquire what my father did for a living. He told me he worked as an engineer at Leaf Brands, Inc., a large manufacturer of candy and gum in Chicago. He explained that he didn't drive a train. No, he was the kind of engineer who worked at fixing things, especially the big machines used in the making of candy and gum. I would overhear him talking to his friends over a card game about a confounded new machine the company was buying and how it kept breaking down. All I knew for sure was that he would come home from work every day smelling of bubble gum, carrying boxes of gumballs and Whoppers and uncut sheets of baseball cards—how bad could that be? I knew at that point that I, too, would be an engineer when I grew up.

It made sense that a career in fixing things might be in my future because of an event that had happened several years earlier, when I was seven years old. My parents were away for a few days, and I was staying with my grandmother. I opened the closet door, and the doorknob came off in my hand. I was afraid I had broken something and hesitantly showed it to my grandmother, who reassured me that it happened all the time and that one day she would have it fixed.

I looked at the doorknob and then at the spindle remaining in the door. Clearly, the knob slipped over the spindle, but how did it stay attached? I noticed there was a little screw on the side of the knob overlying the point at which the spindle entered the knob. I borrowed a screwdriver from my grandma's tool drawer and tightened the screw and *voilà!* the knob was securely attached to the door again.

My grandmother nearly plotzed. What a genius! Only seven years old, and already he's fixing the doorknob! She called my mother long-distance, and my mother started crying with pride. Never mind that Mozart had written umpteen concertos by that age: I had fixed a doorknob! I was beaming. I had done something helpful with my hands, and all the important women in my life were now terribly proud of me. Was it a portent of things to come? Perhaps I, too, destined to become an engineer, fix things, and make women happy.

❖   *Rich Leafs, Other Leafs*

The owners of the candy company had the same last name as we did, and my father told me they were distant cousins. He never was able to explain exactly how we were related, saying that it all got muddied up by the fact that all of them had been born in Russia and immigrated to the United States around 1914. My mother said that they were "high society," that they traveled to Europe and drove fancy cars. "They were the rich Leafs," she said. Even a seven-year-old could figure what that meant for us.

A few years ago, a woman from Palm Springs came to see me for consultation. She asked if I were related to the Leafs of the candy company. I said that I was, but explained that I never knew the exact connection. She said that Minnie Leaf, the aged widow of one of the founding Leafs, lived next door to her in Palm Springs and was her friend. She returned two weeks later with Minnie, age ninety-six, in tow.

I hadn't seen or spoken to Minnie in many years, but I remembered quite fondly. She had always been gracious and interested in my life, and had flown to Detroit from Chicago to attend my wedding (first one). She said she knew the answer to the mystery of our relationship.

"We aren't related," she said sweetly. She explained that her long-deceased husband had emigrated on the same boat from Europe to

New York with my grandfather and his young family and that they all became friends playing pinochle during the crossing. They had never met before, and they had similar but not identical last names (Lifschutz and Lifschitz). They all had their names changed to Leaf when they arrived at Ellis Island.

At that moment, a feeling of liberation swept over me. My family was no longer the poor Leafs. We were just *other* Leafs!

❖   *High School Musical*

School was always easy for me. The public school system in Chicago at that time was still in pretty good shape. The teachers were motivated. Classes were usually interesting, and there was plenty of art and science to learn. Students who went to private schools were usually thought of as *problem* kids. The concept of privilege really didn't enter into my consciousness.

I liked school in general, but I would take any opportunity to blame some nonlethal disease as an excuse to stay home and play or watch television. I soon became interested in reading books, listening to music, making model cars, and watching more television. I took years of piano lessons, practiced when I had to, and found myself coasting through school with ease.

I found that I was pretty good at playing the piano in elementary school. I played at recitals and classroom talent shows, and I became quite friendly with some really talented young musicians. In high school I parlayed my musical interests into a regular gig with a small combo—the kind that played at parties, weddings, and bar mitzvahs. We played from "fake books," ring-bound notebooks with bootleg pages in them, which were probably illegal, though everyone used them. All we needed was the melody line and the chord, and we could "fake it" from there. Piano was my instrument, and I developed some skill at arranging, writing out the notes for the others in the band on blank tablature paper.

Most of my arrangements were simply "covers" for some of the popular recordings of the day. Originality was not a valued commodity at that point. Sounding good and not getting fired was the important thing. Later in my senior year, when I started pairing with a string bass player who loved jazz, I found that a good solid foundation in music theory and proficiency was requisite to being a jazz musician. I had to learn the essentials before I could become really creative, a lesson basic to any art form. I later discovered that this concept could also be applied to the practice of plastic surgery, for a surgeon must know the science, the anatomy, and the surgical skills before he can work on creating something of beauty.

I loved high school. It was a time when incredible optimism and unquestioned patriotism prevailed throughout the country. It was the Eisenhower era, postwar and pre-Vietnam. We all truly believed we could achieve anything we set our hearts on.

Of all my memories, the one I recall most vividly is of that day in the spring of 1957 when *Life* magazine came to South Shore High School and, for some reason that remains inexplicable, chose me to exemplify the typical American high school student. They planned to compare me to a typical Russian high school student. Sputnik had just become the first Earth-orbiting satellite, to worldwide acclaim. The newspapers (remember *them*?) were crying out that we had lost the space race to the Soviets.

The goal of the *Life* piece was to refute the popular notion that the American high schooler had a superior education. They were daring to consider that if the United States was losing the space race to the Soviets, it might mean that education in that godless, Russkie, Communist abyss might actually be even better than ours. But somewhere during the course of prepping the article, they found out that I was *not* your average American student, that I was a pretty smart feller, that my father had actually been born in Russia, and, perhaps most disconcerting for the Luce organization, that I was

Jewish. It would be much better from their point of view to show a more *typical* student.

Nonetheless, I had been picked, and for one glorious day, Stan Wayman, a Pulitzer Prize–winning photojournalist, followed me everywhere with his retinue of assistants. I suddenly was the most popular guy in the school. Everyone wanted to sit with me in the lunchroom, and classmates who never talked to me were accompanying me down the hall to my classrooms while the cameras clicked and whirred around us. Those smugly unapproachable girls were now shyly approaching me! Heady wine, indeed. I was *The Man!*

In the end, they picked another school and another student, one who might have been a model for a character from the TV show *Happy Days*, and I regrettably was once again just *a boy*. The article was a success, and it might well have stimulated the huge surge in science education in the United States that followed. As a consolation prize, they sent me some 11x14 photos, which I have in a box somewhere in my garage. The cruelty of fate: on that one day, my fifteen minutes of fame, I was wearing my nerdy ROTC uniform. It still embarrasses me.

❖ *Michigan: Music or Medicine*

My college experience at the University of Michigan was everything it was supposed to be: living away from my parents, making friends with people whom I never would have met in my own neighborhood, getting drunk once or twice, and most memorably, falling in love and discovering the world of sexual intimacy. I was a living, breathing coming-of-age movie. It was the best time of my life. I also was getting an amazing education.

I think that most college freshmen who claim to know exactly what they want to do when they grow up find that their eventual career choices have little to do with their original plans. I did not have a clearly defined career goal at that time. In retrospect, I see that I must have had some sort of a plan, but at the time it seemed like a random choice. I signed up for a premed curriculum, with a minor in music. Medicine could be a good "fallback" option.

I pledged a fraternity and moved into the house my second year. As was typical of fraternities, many of the members came from wealthy families. Others of us did not. We worked as waiters in the house to help defray our living expenses. I felt no sense of social stigma. We were all *brothers,* and in fact living among the wealthier guys became yet another part of my education.

They were very much into elegant young men's fashion, which meant that more than a few of them had a new wardrobe every fall. I learned about which way the stripes on a rep tie should go, the difference between Ivy League and "Continental" styles, and the fact that a gentleman should never allow a pale hairy leg to show over the top of his socks while he was sitting down. It was long socks with garters or nothing.

Looking back at it now, it's hard not to laugh at this absurd, slavish conformity to a presumably sophisticated style of dress, but those observations weren't completely irrelevant after all. In fact, my interest in how consumers perceive fashion served me well some twenty-five years later when my wife and I owned and operated the Prada boutique in Beverly Hills.

In truth, I lived between two worlds in college, and both were linked by music. I was mostly in synch with the fraternity-sorority thing, my strongest contributions being primarily musical and theatrical. I was the "sing" leader, meaning I led the brothers in rehearsals and serenades when a member became pinned to a girl. I also made a 16mm sound movie for our fraternity-sorority team, one that won first place in the Michigras Spring Festival competition.

The other world was decidedly less Greek and more geek. This was the early '60s just before the Flower Power revolution, and the folk music genre was in full swing. I joined with three other non-Greek (read *hippie*) friends to form a folk quartet at the University of Michigan. Our instruments were diverse: guitar, banjo, mandolin, harmonica, autoharp, Hobo Joe (an odd-looking string bass made from an inverted washtub and a broomstick)—anything that someone in Appalachia, Mississippi, the Caribbean, and even Tudor England might have played, we played. We sang country songs, union songs, drinking songs, protest songs, love songs, and blues. We performed at festivals and almost anywhere we could find a place away from a classroom.

We even performed at fraternity and sorority parties. The odd juxtaposition of beer-swilling fraternity guys and cashmere-sporting sorority girls singing along enthusiastically to "We Shall Overcome" in a house that was definitely off-limits to most minorities remains a bemused memory to me.

Many times after curfew, which was 10:30 PM during the week, we stationed ourselves outside the women's dorms. Fortified against the cold Michigan winter by ill-begotten beer, we sang exuberantly up toward the high-rise windows. We found for our opening number (which was sometimes our closing number if campus security so willed it) that the unmuffled sound of a long-necked, five-string banjo was the best for getting the attention we sought. The girls would fling open their windows and yell requests. They would sometimes pitch their bras or other undergarments down as encouragement. It was an easy way for a shy guy to get the attention of girls.

In the summer of 1961, we traveled around the country in an old VW camper, singing for our supper at various dives and hotels. Over the Fourth of July weekend in Yellowstone National Park, we went table to table in the bar of the Old Faithful Inn, playing requests. We sang "Tom Dooley" over and over until the inherent corniness of it overcame us. I began to understand the difficulties faced by performers with one major hit. For the rest of their performing lives, that would be the one song that they would have to sing every time. Making it sound sincere and fresh each time would be the true test of their abilities.

One of our stops was Kalisa's, a little restaurant on Monterey's Cannery Row, which had a showroom upstairs. Kalisa herself was a big, warmhearted gypsy/hippie woman who loved musicians. She listened to our audition, then offered us dinner and a small room in back to bunk in for the night. We were to be the opening act for her "headliner" that evening. We accepted graciously.

The headliner was a genuine itinerate folksinger/guitarist, not some college boys on a lark for the summer. He was a world-weary weather-beaten man who had actually ridden the rails, who lived out of a small kit bag, and whose guitar was his entire life. He sang his songs from years of experience on the road, not from recordings. He spoke very little about his past, and didn't care to know anything about ours. He was the real article. He also never went anywhere without a pint of whiskey in his hip pocket.

It turned out that we were *all* sharing the room in back, and our headliner made it clear pretty quickly that he had the single bunk, and that he was suspicious of anyone who wasn't interested in destroying themselves by alcohol abuse. To gain his respect, we all took requisite sips from his passed bottle of Jim Beam, bluffed our manly pleasure over it, and did a few warm-up songs with him in the room before the performance.

We did the show and watched his performance: he half-talked, half-sang songs that he drew convincingly from his soul. It was a riveting experience, and made us more aware than ever that we were only pretenders. We all retired to our quarters where there was more pickin' and singin', and more Jim Beam. We were pulling out all our musical performing tricks to gain his admiration and validation. We knew we were pretty hot, and we felt we were opening his eyes to our young enthusiasm and stylistic arrangements.

Before he passed out for the night, having reached a pinnacle of drunkenness and slurred speech, he struggled to his feet and indicated that he was about to give us his critique. We awaited his comments with rapt anticipation. He paused for dramatic effect. As was his manner, his judgment was terse:

"Boys, keep yer day jobs."

During the school year, we often went into Detroit and played at some of the coffeehouses there. In one of those coffeehouses, The Impromptu, one man was sitting with a group of his friends, watching our performance intently. After our set, he invited us over and introduced himself. His name was Mickey Shorr, a famous disc jockey in the Detroit area. We did our best to act unimpressed, but this was *Mickey Shorr!*

He liked our act, and he wanted to talk to us about signing with a record label. Folk music was very hot at the time. Joan Baez, Pete Seeger, the Weavers, Dylan, and Odetta were gaining in popularity, and The Kingston Trio, which we tended to sneer at (so commercial!), were topping the Billboard charts. The Beatles were still a few years away.

Mr. Shorr indicated that he would like to represent us, and he wanted to talk to our parents about signing a contract with him. We were in heaven. Maybe we would be the next young college guys to hit the big time. We were trying to stay focused on schoolwork, but we couldn't help daydreaming about how we would deal with the fame and fortune that would soon be ours.

Maybe I wouldn't be an engineer after all.

Unfortunately for us and even more so for him, Mr. Shorr soon became the second DJ in the country to be fired because of the infamous Payola scandal. In our collective naïveté, we were morally outraged to find out that he had accepted money to play singles on the radio. We had no idea that this was standard operating procedure in the music business of the time and perhaps of all time. More importantly, we were chagrined that our glimpse of stardom had so quickly and so cruelly been brought to a close.

That incident, along with the growing realization that I was at best a mediocre musician, brought me to the decision that music was not to be my future. If I wanted to be able to support myself and possibly a family someday, I would need a more reliable career. The folk music industry was a dead end for me, and engineering didn't look that promising, either. I wanted to do something that involved both art and science, and I liked the idea of helping people who might be appreciative of my efforts.

Perhaps it was by a process of elimination, but a career in medicine seemed like my best choice. I could still enjoy music as an amateur. I applied to several of the best medical schools in the nation, counting on the fact that even though I was only a junior in college, my grades were good enough to get me accepted without a bachelor's degree.

They were, and I was.

❖   *Medical School*

My early interests were in the field of psychiatry, and the University of Chicago Medical School wisely encouraged that discipline during the first two years of the school curriculum. Even though the predominant focus at that time was on the preclinical sciences like anatomy and biochemistry, etc., we were developing experience in the doctor-patient relationship with psychiatry residents as mentors.

It was a wonderfully effective program. We would interview volunteer maternity patients during their regularly scheduled appointments at the Chicago Lying-In Hospital and then discuss the interviews with our psych residents on a weekly basis. We gradually developed awareness of the ways patients related to doctors, and we learned of some of the unspoken clues that were so important in understanding their anxieties and concerns. And we came to realize the enormous weight that our professional words carried, even as medical students.

As time went by, I realized that psychiatry, for all its fascination and insights, was a little too vague for me to accept as my primary vocation. There wasn't a clear defining line between normal and abnormal (a boundary I still find elusive in my practice of plastic surgery). Nor was there *one correct* treatment for any given illness or a point at which one could clearly define a cure. What I gleaned from my experience was essential to the practice of any aspect of medicine— namely, the verbal and nonverbal ways patients communicated with their physicians and vice versa. This training early in my medical school experience reverberates in me every day and with every patient I meet.

My first clinical rotation, starting in my third year, was in surgery, and I came to know Dr. Hilger Perry Jenkins, professor of surgery. Dr. Jenkins was an anomaly at the university. He was primarily a clinician in a setting that was strongly weighted toward basic research. That is, he preferred working with patients rather than test tubes or laboratory animals.

He was a slight man in his late sixties—well past the mandatory retirement age—a gentle, eccentric soul peering over glasses perched on the end of his pointed nose, an unlit, partially chewed cigarette in his pocket and a persistent twinkle in his eyes. He had stopped smoking several years before because of a heart ailment, but he kept the cigarette available to stave off the urge to smoke. He always wore an old, double-breasted, blue serge suit. I never once saw him wearing the ubiquitous white coat that everyone from students to professors wore. It just wasn't his style. I believe that he was tolerated by some of the staff as an oddity more than respected as a surgeon.

Dr. Jenkins was a general surgeon by training and profession, but he had scaled down his surgical schedule, preferring the smaller, less stressful operations. Though he had once been a noted gastrointestinal surgeon doing quite extended abdominal surgery, he now had become the de facto plastic surgeon, mostly because none of the other members of the surgical staff were interested in things like skin tumors, burn treatment, and breast reconstruction after mastectomy. Besides, there were no trained plastic surgeons on the staff of the University of Chicago at that time.

He was the surgeon of choice for cleft-lip repair. (He referred to it by its old-fashioned, now politically incorrect term, "harelip" because of the rabbit-like appearance.) I think that most of the surgery staff members were more typical of what one commonly thinks of as a surgeon: bold, macho men doing big, blood-and-guts, lifesaving surgery. Anything less was "minor" surgery.

On Sundays, Dr. Jenkins would show up at the hospital, telling his wife he was off to church. This was what he called his "Sunday ecclesiastical clinic," during which time he would see many patients on his own, without any nursing staff or clerks around to help him. I spent a lot of time hanging out with Dr. Jenkins, learning things that are not often described in a book. Mostly, I learned from the way he respectfully cared for his patients, many of whom could not afford to pay for a regular clinic visit—hence, the bootlegged Sunday hours. His was the personal touch, and his patients adored him.

Eight years later, near the end of my residency and long after Dr. Jenkins had retired, I was working in the emergency room when an ambulance brought in a DOA. It was an old man in a rumpled blue suit, with a wet cigarette in his pocket. He was gone—the victim of a sudden heart attack. It was my job and sad obligation to his death certificate.

In spite of the many powerful, widely respected, and famed surgeons whom I studied under at the university, it was this modest man who had given me the most important lesson. *It is an incredible gift to be able to help patients in need.* My signature would now remain on the closing page of his book, but his imprint would remain as a basic tenet in my training for the rest of my life.

During my final two years of medical school, I found myself becoming increasingly interested in surgery as a career. The indications for treatment were clear. The therapy was precise and incisive (no pun intended), the recovery finite, and the results, good or bad, clearly apparent. Plus, I got to use my hands and the logical, rational, Virgo side of my brain. (An interesting observation: an inordinate number of the plastic surgeons I have worked with over the years have been Virgos, like me.) There was also a fascination with the heroic aspects of being able to save a life or cure an illness through my own feats of skill and daring.

Of all the surgical subspecialties, none was more dramatically perched at the life-death interface than cardiac surgery. When I graduated from medical school, I set my sights on becoming a heart surgeon. I was fortunate to match up for a rotating surgical internship (serving on different surgical specialties each month) at Stanford, my first choice, where the cardiac surgery program was among the best in the country. I soon found that not everything turns out as planned.

❖ *Learning the Skills*

My internship at Stanford started on July 1, 1966, and my first rotation was cardiac surgery. It was a most humbling experience. As absorbed as I was by the wondrous intricacies and drama of seeing a beating heart opened and repaired like some machine (and it is *some machine*), I found that I wasn't doing very well as an intern. Although I had graduated third in my class from the University of Chicago and had been a member of Alpha Omega Alpha (medical school equivalent of Phi Beta Kappa), I simply was not yet catching on to the drill.

The scholarly discussions of medical school weren't going to get the post-op patient through the night. That required endless scut work, task organization, and tireless attention to details. Electrolytes, blood gasses, chest tube maintenance, tracheal suction, anticoagulant levels—there was no time for the luxury of thought, reflection, or sleep. Others in my internship class seemed to get into the required routine much more readily than I could. If that had been my fifth or sixth month's rotation, it might have been different. Perhaps I would have been more "in the groove" and ended up as a cardiac surgeon after all.

"Maybe you should consider a career in psychiatry" is perhaps the most humiliating insult that an attending surgeon can fling at a struggling intern or resident. I began to think that perhaps that was meant for me. Surgery, so far, did not seem to be my strong suit.

My second month's rotation was in the plastic surgery service, and things began looking up. Dr. Robert Chase was chairman of both the department of surgery and the department of plastic surgery. He was a warm, charismatic educator and a superb surgeon. He had a particular interest in reconstructive hand surgery and drew referrals from all over the western United States and Mexico. He saw patients whose hands had been mangled and maimed in various ways, but there was a particular group of hand injuries that were of special interest in his practice—hands injured by homemade bombs.

These were not the hands of radical fundamentalists or revolutionaries. They were kids, teenagers usually, who tried to make a bomb just for the stupid fun of it. Pipe bombs, roll bombs, tin can bombs, and rockets—all stunts that went tragically wrong. One young man had lost both eyes and both thumbs. Imagine the damage if more potent explosives had been available.

Hand surgery was creative. It was exciting, and it worked. The loss of a thumb is a most debilitating injury, because of the need to oppose the fingers and grasp items such as a key or a pencil. I learned the innovative techniques required to make an opposable, working thumb from an index finger. In some cases, when there was a complete loss of the base of the thumb, one could create a thumb from a bone graft and cover it with a flap of soft tissue. Then, to make the thumb truly workable, a flap of innervated tissue from the side of an adjacent finger was carefully transferred to the new thumb to give it sensation: it wouldn't work unless there was feeling in it.

Seeing a young man's joy in the simple act of picking up a fork and feeding himself, of reestablishing a lost sense of autonomy, was thrilling indeed. I learned from my patients that the ultimate test of successful hand rehabilitation was the ability to pick up and drink from a paper cup without crushing it. But it wasn't until I helped take care of a baby with a cleft lip and palate did I know that plastic surgery was my future.

Congenital anomalies are accidents of embryonic development. Most of them occur within the first trimester of pregnancy when all the organ systems are being formed. Between the tenth and twelfth week of development, the two separate buds that become the jaws and mouth are brought together in the midline and fuse. When this does not work out exactly as designed (about one in 750 live births), a cleft will result. This may be only the upper lip, or it may include the gums and the hard and soft palate as well.

The ensuing deformity in a newborn baby is a heartbreaking event for the parents. It is frequently associated with other chronic problems, including an inability to nurse, developmental speech impairments, ear infections, and dental abnormalities, but the immediate problem is the horrifying appearance. In other times in other countries, babies with clefts were left alone to die, but in our fortunate time and place, we have the ability to restore an infant to near-normalcy in most cases.

The surgical techniques involved with repairing a cleft lip or palate are often intricate, and they leave scars; however, the improvement is transformational. The incredible happiness I felt when anxious parents were handed back their precious child, looking like a *normal* baby, was indescribable.

I was hooked. I finally knew where I wanted to go with my career. I had not yet seen one face-lift, one nose job, one breast augmentation. I was aware that plastic surgery included some "beauty" surgery, but that was not my goal.

Back to the University of Chicago I went. Dr. Harvey Zarem had just completed his plastic surgery training at Johns Hopkins, and he was looking for his first resident to begin the new program at the University of Chicago. If I wanted it, that could be me. I jumped at the opportunity. California would have to wait.

Residency training in general surgery is a prerequisite to most plastic surgery programs. The ensuing six years as a general surgery and plastic surgery resident are a blur in retrospect. At the time, it was an endless sentence—six bloody years of hard labor. It was nights on end of zero sleep, staggering responsibility for the care of multiple patients with varying degrees of illness, reading up on the next morning's surgical procedure, presenting complications at the weekly M&M (morbidity and mortality) conferences and confessing your errors, being called on the carpet for every perceived flaw in patient management, and inevitably being fired once or twice by the attending surgeon.

During my residency, I rotated through all of the surgery services, and among other things, I became chief resident in surgery, plastic surgery, and pediatric surgery. I spent many memorable months as surgical resident in the emergency room.

The ER was the epicenter of acute medicine and surgery. The fragility and strength of the human body and spirit were on vivid display, especially between about 9:00 PM and 5:00 AM. There was an almost predictable ebb and flow of activity. Early in the evening came the sick folks with flu and pneumonia who didn't have their own doctors and used the ER as their own urgent care system. Much later, in the wee hours of the morning came the ladies of the night, walking with the characteristic painful gait typical of pelvic inflammatory disease caused by gonorrhea. In between, from about 9:00 PM until 2:00 AM or so, were the essentials of the nighttime surgical residency training: gunshot wounds.

The University of Chicago was (and is) located on the south side of Chicago. What once had been a large, upscale, elegant neighborhood had retreated to an enclave of higher learning and sophistication surrounded on three sides by an ongoing gang rivalry, the fourth side being Lake Michigan. Because it was a widely esteemed center for research and education, surgery residents and their medical students would alternate between nonparallel universes.

By day, we were working on inflammatory bowel disease, non-Hodgkin's lymphoma, and the immunologic basis of tissue transplantation. By night, the gangs kept the ER very busy: "Saturday night special" gunshot wounds, stabbings, and automobile accidents. The "Woodlawn Rod and Gun Club" was the metaphor for the bloody attack-and-retaliate state of gang warfare between the Blackstone Rangers and the Devil's Disciples.

Besides the fallout of the gang wars, I saw children who had sustained horrific burns by being immersed in tubs of scalding water by their parents as punishment for being naughty. I saw nightstick-inflicted head injuries during the 1968 Democratic convention riots. I saw a young woman found in a coal bin with fourteen bullets in her body and head, who signed herself out of the hospital AMA (against medical advice) a few days later. I personally witnessed an amazing variety of *objects* that somehow found their way into men's rectums, and I was there for the famously tragic Illinois Central train wreck in which more than two hundred people died.

That day, I had to crawl under the wreckage and start an IV in the motorman who had been asleep at the wheel while we waited for the heavy equipment that could free him. The fact that he was pinned in a position *above* me made it tricky; neither water nor IV fluids can run uphill.

At the time, I felt that the traditional arrangement of two years of plastic surgery training *after* completion of four to five years training in general surgery was overly rigorous and redundant. The purpose of that seemingly endless boot camp became clear only in retrospect. Learning how to perform an operation is one thing, but having the comfort level, the experience, the judgment to perform the operation safely and expertly, and the ability to calmly deal with any unforeseen events is totally different.

There is an indefinable sense of confidence that one gains from many years of study and training, of stress and backbreaking struggle, of numbing, humbling on-the-job experiences. Even with the relatively safe aesthetic procedures that I now specialize in, both my patients and I are comforted by the knowledge that I can handle virtually anything that might happen during or after the surgical procedure. I doubt that dermatologists or dentists who advertise themselves as "cosmetic surgeons" have or can instill that level of confidence.

❖ *A Lesson in Humility*

The flip side of confidence can be and often is cockiness, and no one is cockier than a graduating chief resident; he or she has seen it all, done it all, and knows it all. That attitude lasts until the umbrella of a residency program is gone, and the real work of medical care has begun. There was an incident just before end of my training that brought me crashing back to earth, and quickly.

During my chief residency in plastic surgery, a fourteen-year-old girl was brought by her mother to the University of Chicago Cleft Palate Clinic from a small town in downstate Illinois. Wendy had been raised on a farm. She was a sweet, shy teenager, somewhat uncomfortable with the big city hospital setting. She had long, straight, light brown hair, beautiful eyes, and a ready smile. She was being seen for treatment of a variant of cleft palate called Pierre-Robin syndrome, marked externally by a very small chin, a large nose, and a pronounced speech defect.

At first glance, it appeared that her palate was normal, but listening to her speak for a few seconds was enough to make a diagnosis of velopharyngeal incompetence. This was a situation that often occurred in patients with cleft palates, or in Wendy's case, submucous cleft palate (the palate looks outwardly normal, but there is a lack of fusion of the muscle underneath the mucous membranes). In either case, the soft palate does not rise and move backward well enough during speech to block the flow of air from the windpipe through the nose. Certain speech sounds, especially *plosives* like "p" and "b," require that all the air be directed through the mouth and none be allowed to escape through the nose. (You can try this yourself. Say "peanut butter" while you let the air out your nose on every sound.)

Although Wendy's outward appearance was slightly abnormal, it was not in any sense freakish or debilitating. Her real disability was in speech. Other teenagers laughed at her and said that she sounded like a duck. She became noncommunicative and began to experience problems in school.

Our initial goal was to improve her speaking ability, and perhaps we would address her appearance at a later time. Because cleft palate surgery was what had initially caught my interest in plastic surgery, I was enthusiastic about the procedure.

In Wendy's case, the plan was to do a common surgical procedure called a pharyngeal flap. In this operation, a piece of tissue from the back wall of the throat is sutured to a similar piece of tissue from the soft palate, creating a permanent bridge. This decreases the amount of air escaping through the nose during speech and allows the previously inadequate palate to close the nasal airway more completely during orally created sounds.

The operation worked beautifully. Wendy returned home. Her speech and her grades improved, and she became much more confident. The major goal had been met and exceeded.

Toward the final weeks of my residency, her mother asked if we could finish the job by improving her appearance. I was very excited at the opportunity to complete the ugly-duckling-to-swan transformation. We saw her in the clinic and planned her operation: The small chin would be enlarged by means of a chin implant, and at the same time, she would have a rhinoplasty to reshape and reduce her nose. It was the perfect combination, an uncomplicated and mostly "routine" case.

Wendy's operation proceeded without incident. The operation was done under general anesthesia, using an endotracheal tube that went into the trachea through the mouth to provide an airway. In Wendy's case, the intubation (insertion of the tube) was somewhat tricky, because the anatomy of her throat had been altered by her previous pharyngeal flap operation; however, the anesthesiologist was up to the task, and the entire operation went smoothly. At the end of the procedure, the nose and chin appeared in balance, and she actually looked pretty. The dressings were placed, and she was awakened and brought into the recovery room.

What happened after that only became clear in retrospect.

About twenty minutes after she had entered the recovery room, she stopped breathing and sustained a complete cardiac arrest. There are many reasons this might have happened in a postoperative patient, and most of them are completely preventable today. But at that time, our warnings came too late. CPR was begun immediately, and the anesthesia team tried valiantly to establish an airway by reinserting an endotracheal tube. When several attempts were unsuccessful, perhaps because of the altered anatomy of her throat, I performed an emergency tracheotomy in order to get a direct airway to her lungs, but it was too late. Despite continued heroic attempts at CPR, Wendy died that day.

Surgeons are supposed to be rather cool in the face of death. It is bad enough having to explain to a parent the death of a beloved child with terminal malignancy or severe trauma or illness (perhaps this was why I had difficulty with heart surgery). It was much, much worse having to tell Wendy's mother that her daughter had passed away after a *nose job.*

Any cockiness I had once had vanished. Even now, thirty-five years later, I can recall the feelings of helplessness I had endured that day. The lesson of Wendy's death is simple: there's no such thing as a "routine" case. The corollary to that statement seems counterintuitive, but it is the plastic surgeon's credo: the responsibility for protecting a patient's life and well-being is even more sacred in elective cosmetic surgery than in lifesaving major surgical procedures.

I'll never forget her.

❖ *Learning the Art*

"See one, do one, teach one," was and still is the half-serious mantra of surgical training programs worldwide. Residents learn their skills by means of a graduated level of responsibility. They ascend from second assistant to first assistant to chief resident to instructor, and there is no joking about the responsibility for the patient's well-being.

This is a constant dilemma in the training programs. No patient should ever be placed in harm's way by being in the care of an untrained surgeon, yet there is always a point when novice surgeons must have at least some responsibility for the patient's care. A good training program offers and requires a step-by-step increase in surgical skill and responsibility. Determining when a surgeon is finally "good to go" on his own, without a supervisory safety net, is a difficult moral, legal, and educational struggle.

We place our faith in guidelines established by the government and organized medicine so that when a resident finishes formal training, he or she should be capable of operating safely and effectively within a given area of expertise. Competency is further ensured by successfully passing the written and oral certifying exam of the appropriate American board—in my case, the American Board of Plastic Surgery—but as Mike Gurdin, my mentor, once said in his uniquely Arkansasian fashion, "Board certification is like a fishin' license. You've gotta have it, but it doesn't mean you'll catch a fish."

Simply because a doctor has had proper training and board certification doesn't mean he or she is an exceptionally adept surgeon. It takes more than proper training and board certification to develop a successful practice. Much of this training may come well *after* the finish of formal training programs.

In view of what I do in my practice today, it seems odd that I never did a single face-lift in my residency training. Plastic surgery was new to the University of Chicago when I began my residency, and the new chief was struggling with the established bureaucracy to carve out a specialty. He did very well at establishing *reconstructive* surgery training, but when it came to getting aesthetic surgery experience, it just wasn't happening at the university. Consequently, he did what modern companies do with some of their services: he "outsourced" me to a busy suburban private practice.

At this practice, I met with doctors who had their offices in nice, modern buildings, who drove upscale cars to various hospitals to perform their work, and who had a well-integrated social and family life. This was different from the university, where offices, clinics, and hospitals were under one all-inclusive vast umbrella, where there was as much or more emphasis placed on research than on patient care, and where stress of the "publish or perish" mantra was pervasive.

The private practice doctors didn't wear white coats but well-tailored suits and ties. They expected to get paid for their services, and they were. The "town vs. gown" battle lines were very clearly drawn. Yet they did participate voluntarily in the training of residents at the University of Illinois Medical School, one of them even being the chief of the program. I cherished some of the academic traditions at the University of Chicago, but suddenly my eyes were open to a balance I could happily live with.

When I finished my residency, I was offered two career choices. The University of Illinois offered me the plum job of full-time chief of the cleft palate / craniofacial surgery clinic. They would pay me to go to Paris for a year and study with Dr. Paul Tessier, the gifted and innovative plastic surgeon who had revolutionized the treatment of children with severe craniofacial deformities. These were children much more severely deformed than mere cleft lips or palates, and Dr. Tessier was restoring them to substantial degrees of normalcy. Operations were performed with neurosurgeons as part of the team, because some of the surgery was done from *inside* the skull. It was very daring, and Dr. Tessier's legacy is seen today at every plastic surgery department around the world.

The other opportunity was less academically exciting but more interesting in other ways. My chief of plastic surgery had just accepted a job as the chief of the department at UCLA, and he encouraged me to come along. I could be on the clinical faculty and have a private practice, but I would have to live in the Los Angeles area—you know, palm trees, beaches, great weather, convertibles, The Rose Bowl. It was a difficult choice. It took me about fifteen minutes. *California, here I come ...* again.

My first experience in the practice of plastic surgery was at the Kaiser-Permanente Hospital in Hollywood. It was a perfect place to get my "sea legs." The day I moved my pictures onto my own desk in my own office, I had *a practice.* I even had a secretary and a nurse, and patients were waiting for me—for *me*! And I had a liveable salary! How does someone get so lucky?

The transition from residency to a financially workable practice was an eye-opener. Although I had earned a meager salary as a resident, my only experience at receiving money directly related to taking care of patients had been as a senior medical student. I was assigned to the ER at one point, and a man came in with complete urinary obstruction from a large prostate, an extremely painful experience. The ER resident was very busy, and he told me to go ahead and pass a catheter into his bladder. I did it and relieved his obstruction and his pain instantly. The patient was so grateful that he wrote out a personal check to me for one hundred dollars.

What to do? I was only a student, very intent on making good grades and doing the right thing. And a hundred bucks was *a lot*. But students weren't supposed to be earning money at school; they were supposed to be paying it, as tuition.

As it happened, one of my senior professors was walking through the ER on his way out of the hospital. I stopped him and asked him what to do. Dr. Walter Lincoln Palmer was one of the preeminent gastroenterologists at the university, known and highly esteemed worldwide for his research on the medical treatment of ulcers.

"Cash it quick," he replied without breaking his stride and continued past me out of the building.

At Kaiser I was doing all kinds of reconstructive surgery, and what made me happiest was that I was the plastic surgeon for the cleft palate team. Kaiser drew from a population of several million patients, and with the frequency of clefts being approximately one in every 750 live births, we were busy. The team had a pediatrician, an ear, nose, and throat doctor, a speech pathologist, a dentist, a prosthodontist, a social worker, and a plastic surgeon (me). We would meet once a week and review five to six cases, each individual offering his or her expertise to create a well-conceived therapeutic plan.

On Thursday evenings I would go to Journal Club at UCLA with the UCLA full-time staff and the clinical faculty, the surgeons in private practice who voluntarily joined in the training of residents at the university. This was where the surgeons would talk about real cases but also about restaurants, sports, vacations, and cars, among other things. The barrier between the town and gown doctors seemed very unsubstantial in that setting. It was there I learned that Dr. Michael Gurdin was looking for a junior associate to help him in his practice.

My ears pricked up. Mike Gurdin? He was one of the most respected names in the field, nationally and internationally. He had just completed his term as president of the American Society of Aesthetic Plastic Surgeons, and years earlier, as a resident, I had presented a paper in Montreal at the meeting of the American Society of Plastic and Reconstructive Surgeons, the "Big" society, with Mike Gurdin presiding over that august organization. He was looking for a junior guy? This was a major opportunity. I called the next day.

Mike met me in his office, and he welcomed me warmly. He was a striking man with a beautiful shock of silver hair and the persistence of a Southern drawl, and he wore a black shirt open at the collar and black pants. *So this is how successful doctors dress in Los Angeles,* I presumed. My upbringing was much more conservative, and I couldn't picture myself in anything so *Hollywood*. (Just a fluke, as it turned out. I never saw him later without a jacket and tie.)

I mentioned to him that I had met him several years earlier when I had decided to move to Los Angeles, and my chief had introduced me around to the LA surgeons. Mike had no recollection of that meeting. This set me back, thinking that I must have been very unmemorable. Now, thirty years later, I have met so many young plastic surgeons trying to find an opportunity in Beverly Hills that I understand his lapse. He did indicate that he was happy to meet me (again), but he had already agreed to bring in another young surgeon whom I knew. I was too late. I thanked him and left. Perhaps Kaiser would be my ultimate destiny.

Several Sundays later, I was working in my yard, trying to plant some green shrubbery in the adobe clay soil native to the Los Angeles area, when he called me at home. His plans with the other doctor weren't working out, mainly because the other doctor was being insistent on building an operating room in the office, and Mike did not like the idea. At that time, neither Mike nor I had any idea that in a few years virtually all aesthetic surgery would be performed in outpatient surgicenters, many of them in doctor's offices. It was fortunate for me that all my experience up to then had been in a hospital setting, for he and I shared the same point of view.

He asked me if I could come over that afternoon. I tried not to look too eager. About an hour later, I was in his home in Beverly Hills, high on a hillside with an amazing view of the city. We were sitting beside the pool, and his wife, Marlene, came out to offer me a drink. She was quite a bit younger than Mike, tall, thin, and gorgeous, wearing a tiny bikini and a great big smile. I was being snowed, and I was loving it.

I joined Mike's practice in stages. I decided to hedge my bets and continue half-time at Kaiser to make sure I had some income, and I worked with Mike two and a half days a week. I would assist him in surgery and take his night and weekend calls. He would pay me a small stipend and try to steer some patients my way. He said that he was eliminating breast surgery from his practice because he felt that "women are pickier about their bosoms than they are about their faces." As a result, he would refer breast patients to me.

It took a few months before I cut the cord at Kaiser completely, and a few short years later, Mike and I were partners. As he was slowing down, I was building up steam, and it couldn't have been better if I planned it that way. Mike retired about nine years after I had joined him. He continued to consult and defend plastic surgeons against frivolous malpractice cases in court as an expert witness.

He loved to hunt and fish, and years later he was on a fishing trip in Oregon with his son when he had a stroke that ultimately led to his death. He was a most beloved man, surgeon, and teacher. He was my mentor about everything in aesthetic surgery, both in and out of the operating room.

After my formal training, my board certification (my "fishing license"), it was Mike who taught me the art and craft of aesthetic plastic surgery. He warned me about the patient who flatters too much, about the patient who complains about every other doctor (see *Mrs. Wong from Hong Kong*), and about the patient who is much too concerned over the minutest details. He would often say, "Norm, God almighty can't make this patient happy, and it's for damn sure I'm not gonna either!"

He taught me the simple gift of adjusting fees (eliminating) for certain needy patients, and even with some of the wealthiest patients in the world, he showed me the importance of fair and appropriate fees. "Never try to get rich on one patient," he often said. In the art and the craft of plastic surgery, I learned at the feet of the master.

And now, here I am, more than thirty years later, practicing in the center of the most vanity-driven youth culture in the world. My training, my experience, and my time spent with wonderful mentors have prepared me for success in that undertaking. I love the creativity, the energy, and the sanctity of the operating room. I love seeing the fruits of my labors in the smoother faces, the brighter eyes, and the uplifted spirits of my patients. It is an honor and a thrill every day to come to work and do what I do.

But it is also a daily struggle to explain the reality of plastic surgery to hopeful patients, some of whom have stars in their eyes from watching too many TV shows, some of whom are desperate to reverse results of previous botched surgeries, some of whom are hoping to save their marriage, some of whom are clutching at fame, and some of whom have serious emotional disorders. They all have a dream, and my job is to see if plastic surgery can play a part in helping them fulfill that dream.

CHAPTER TWO
THE UNIQUE JOYS OF PRACTICING IN BEVERLY HILLS

I practice in Beverly Hills. If I had practiced in Chicago, my patients might have been involved in the world of commodities and banking. In New York, they could likely have been in securities trading and arbitrage. In Seattle, perhaps computers and aircraft. In Houston or Dallas, maybe oil and gas. In Los Angeles and especially in Beverly Hills (did you know that Beverly Hills is a completely separate city, entirely surrounded by Los Angeles?), the industry of the area is by and large the entertainment business, so it's not surprising that many of my patients are intimately connected to it.

This doesn't mean that they are all movie stars. Some are. Most are not. They may be producers, directors, writers, cinematographers, musicians, set designers, costumers, studio executives, grips, drivers, stuntmen, donut salesmen—or perhaps even their wives or husbands, sons or daughters, assistants or maids.

Or mistresses ... I've done many operations on beautiful single women who appear to be unemployed and whose bills are paid from unnamed accounts administered by well-known business attorneys. I suppose they could be heiresses on trust funds, but you get a feeling about these things after a few years in the Platinum Triangle.

For the most part, catering to this crowd does make for interesting, unusual experiences. I recall the internationally known actress who insisted on scheduling her surgery on a date that most astrologically matched *both* our horoscopes and then brought in a large crystal to place under the operating table for its healing energy. Also memorable was the famous TV producer who wanted to hear the soundtrack to his recently cancelled series while I removed a skin cancer from his forehead. He wanted to associate the negative energy of the two different issues and somehow cancel them out. There was the struggling bit-part actor who wore a full disguise (with wig) to consult with me, while an Oscar-winning leading lady was sitting openly and comfortably in the waiting room nearby, chatting up my receptionist; and many, many actors who insisted that I watch them on a videotape or DVD to see how they looked *while they were performing.*

There are some drawbacks to practicing in a celebrity-oriented area. Once a face-lift patient tried to sue me because she felt that she no longer looked like Elizabeth Taylor, a resemblance she had previously parlayed into many celebrity look-alike contests. Pointing out to her that Elizabeth Taylor herself no longer looked like Elizabeth Taylor did not diminish her disappointment and subsequent anger. Her attempted lawsuit was dropped when she found that no reasonable attorney would represent her.

Another time quite early in my career, I consulted with a pair of tall, beautiful, Amazon-like actress-model twins who were to star in a new Las Vegas review. They suggested that if I would perform breast augmentation on them and let them pay my fees and expenses over a six-month period, they would refer all their friends in the Vegas showgirl community to me. This was appealing to me at the time, having recently begun a solo practice and looking to make it successful.

Alas, my rude awakening came quickly. The day after the sutures were removed, they disappeared, never to be heard from again. No one in the Las Vegas review they were to star in had heard of them.

Even their mother swore that she had no idea where they had flown to. A good friend of mine, an outspoken, aggressive litigating attorney, swore he would "repossess their tits." But no one could find them. I'd been conned by experts.

❖   *The Public Wants to Know*

There are fourteen surgicenters in my building, mostly specializing in plastic surgery. A similar but lesser situation exists in the building directly across the street. As a result, a small pod of paparazzi are always encamped in front of the two medical buildings, waiting for celebs to enter. Once one has entered the building, text messages are sent out to the network, and within minutes the ranks of onlookers swell to crowd proportions. The closer the celeb is to A-list status, the larger the group. By the time the Famous One exits the building, they have to run or at least saunter through a gauntlet of hustling, shouting, strobe-flashing paparazzi to get to the waiting car. All that's missing is a red carpet. And any sense of privacy.

Most plastic surgeons respect their patients' need for privacy. I've done surgery at odd hours to accommodate a publicity-phobic patient who felt much more secure with Sunday or nighttime surgery. My surgicenter also has a side door that opens discreetly into an enclosed loading zone tucked away from the paparazzi's prying telephoto lenses. Privacy is lost when fame is found.

It's no surprise that celebrities who are open and warm in the privacy of my office adopt a no-eye-contact attitude in restaurants or other public settings. This is understandable. If they don't want anyone to see that they know me, which might imply they know me on an other-than-social basis, that's their privilege. To be fair, I think that most times they don't even recognize me without my white coat, out of my office. I'm not all that noticeable.

I've seen every possible means of public denial of plastic surgery. One of my celebrity patients was on the *Tonight Show*, talking to

Johnny Carson about how rested he felt after several weeks at home recovering from a hernia operation. I smiled to myself, knowing that I had done his face-lift the past month. Another celebrity, a famous beauty, was offering that although she's never had plastic surgery, she certainly would if she felt she needed it. Hmmm—*she needed it last year ... and I did it* .

People often even deny to *themselves* that they've had plastic surgery, or at least they minimize it. When I take a history from new patients, I ask them about any prior surgeries they may have had. They may list everything except the obvious nose job in the middle of their faces. If I ask them about it, they respond that they'd simply forgotten to mention it. Probably true, and fair enough.

It also seems that people don't like to own up to the term "face-lift." They usually recall that they had a "minilift" or a "chin tuck" when I can see clearly by the scars that it was, plainly and simply, a face-lift.

Protecting patients' privacy is a ticklish situation, especially with high-profile cases. Many tactics have been devised to prevent the public, particularly the tabloid press, from learning of a celebrity's surgery. Most cosmetic surgery in California is now done in freestanding outpatient surgicenters, which may be part of a doctor's offices. As such, there are fewer people who need to know and fewer chances of leaks than there would be in a hospital.

When I began working with Dr. Gurdin in 1974, all surgery was done in a hospital. To protect identities, his nurse, Dottie Henderson, had a short list of aliases she would rotate through when famous patients were admitted for lab tests or X-rays. Many women were given the name of Joan Newman, a presumably fictitious person. It was a surprisingly effective procedure. Even one of the most recognizable screen icons could go into the hospital wearing sunglasses and no makeup, and get away with it—or so it seemed. The only hitch might occur when, recovering from surgery in a medicated state, the patient forgot his or her assigned name. Fortunately, no serious harm ever resulted from that confusion.

It's important to remember that those were the days when the media still respected privacy. (Think Kennedy's escapades vs. Clinton's.) That's all changed now—any part of a celebrity's life, especially something as juicy as plastic surgery, is fair game for media exploitation.

With the recent scandalous events surrounding the death of Michael Jackson, a great deal of negative publicity has been directed at the use of pseudonyms, particularly when a doctor is prescribing drugs such as painkillers. Up to now, it was not beneath the standard of practice for plastic surgeons to provide fake names to the pharmacy to avoid revealing the true identities of patients in order to protect their images. Although this was always of dubious legality, it has only recently became a serious problem because of the widespread abuse of painkillers. A secretly addicted patient could work the system by asking different doctors to prescribe Vicodan or Percocet under different aliases. The doctors or pharmacists might not catch onto the scheme until it got out of control.

State regulatory boards have now clamped down on the practice. Now we must trust our pharmacists for their discretion as well as their skills.

❖ *Marilyn*

A few years ago, when I began to realize what enormous bills I was paying to the firm that stored our old medical records, I decided the time had come to go through and discard some of those old files. The legal requirements were a little fuzzy, but the commonly accepted reading of the law required that old patient charts be kept for at least seven years. Because I was the custodian of records from Dr. Gurdin's practice, which began around 1945, there was some serious winnowing to do. I had ten boxes of charts at a time brought into the office, and I instructed my staff to be on the lookout for a few specific patients or types of patients. For example, I wanted to keep records on any patients who had received breast implants, because the follow-up on that was important.

I also mentioned that if they came across Marilyn Monroe's chart, then they should bring it to me—and quietly.

Dr. Gurdin had mentioned to me casually over the years that Marilyn had been a patient of his and that he had seen her shortly before she died. I was curious to see if any more specific information was available about this fascinating woman. There was and is today highly voluble speculation and even anger from some individuals who take a proprietary interest in her, plastic surgery or otherwise. Consequently, my next comments here might anger some people and might be disbelieved by others. They are unlikely to resolve any of the contentious arguments about either her plastic surgery or the cause of her death. I'm not one readily open to conspiracy theories, but after reading several books on the subject, I am convinced that there are important questions about her alleged suicide which will never be answered.

The chart was found, and I have it under lock and key. It doesn't have *all* the information that the most avidly curious person would want to know about Marilyn. It is *not* the medical chart that was created during the time of her plastic surgery in 1950. The chart I have was created on July 14, 1958, when she revisited Dr. Gurdin for evaluation of her "flat chin." In Dr. Gurdin's handwriting, a reference is made to a procedure in 1950, in which he and Dr. John Pangman had performed a chin implant on her. The implants of that time were made of carved bovine (from a cow) cartilage. Neither silicone chin implants nor breast implants had not yet been invented.

Dr. Gurdin observed that the implant had slowly reabsorbed, which was typical of that type of graft. He could not palpate any remaining cartilage under the skin of the chin. He did note the persistence of the small scar under the chin through which the implant had been inserted.

No mention is made in that document of her nose, but Dr. Gurdin had told me several times that he and Dr. Pangman had also performed a tip rhinoplasty on her. This would explain the obvious difference between her early photos as Norman Jean Baker and her later more glamorous appearance. (A *tip rhinoplasty* refers to the reshaping of the cartilaginous portions of the nasal tip. The bones of the upper part of the nose are *not* fractured in this type of operation.)

Included in the chart is an envelope containing X-rays of her facial bones taken on June 7, 1962, shortly before her untimely death. The reason for obtaining it, which is explained in the last entry in the chart, was to rule out any facial bone fractures. Nurse Dottie Henderson had obviously reached into her short list of names and had sent Miss Joan Newman to the radiologist's office. Miss Newman's home address on the X-ray is *12305 Fifth Helena, LA 49,* which is widely known as Marilyn's final home. The X-ray report makes no mention of any fractures of the nasal or facial bones.

Out of my own inquisitiveness, I recently asked a radiologist colleague of mine to review the films with me. When he saw the date-stamp, he asked if this was a medical-legal issue. Why else would someone want to review an X-ray that was forty-seven years old?

"Just curious," I replied. I didn't reveal the true identity of the subject.

Using the "bright-light" and magnification, he immediately spotted a minute fracture of the tip of the nasal bone, something that was not mentioned in the original report. No matter ... in a nasal fracture such as this, where there is no displacement of the bone fragments, no treatment would have been required. He also could see no evidence of any other facial fractures.

Although it is only a cold, clinical view of a facial skeleton, it is a picture of Marilyn's face which has been seen by only three or four individuals—a very rare one indeed. The same cannot be said of Joan Newman's name, which appeared over and over again on many of Dr. Gurdin's patients of those golden years. Despite her international fame and iconic sexuality, Marilyn was just one of many to bear that alias.

Marilyn was one of the most beautiful and appealing women ever to grace the silver screen. It's no mystery that she remains to this day—fifty years later—the ultimate symbol of feminine beauty and sex appeal. The fact that she had some small alterations to her face has little to do with her incredible legacy.

❖   *So, What's the Truth about These Beautiful People?*

The public has always wanted to know which of its entertainment idols, including Marilyn, have had plastic surgery. The Internet is jammed with blogs about celebrity plastic surgery that mostly relish in pointing out the worst possible results. The democracy of the Internet is at its grandest and most perverse in these chat rooms and blogs. *Everyone* seems to be an expert on who did or did not have surgical enhancement, and many vehemently and derisively critique the work or other bloggers' opinions.

Here's the truth: By a process of natural selection, most of our celebrities are *born beautiful*. They are aberrations of nature. That's how they (or their parents) gravitated to Hollywood in the first place. ("You are so beautiful. You ought to be in the movies/on TV/modeling/performing.") But once in the spotlight, the dream weavers of the industry conspire to enlarge, reduce, lengthen, brighten, straighten, narrow, bulk up, or otherwise make these already remarkable-looking people *extraordinary*.

The Golden Age of Hollywood was not so golden for the performers: it was more a time when the studio chiefs virtually *owned* the actors. Nowadays if a boss suggests that an employee avoid showing his or her tattoos in public, the employee may file a lawsuit, citing something like "personal expression discrimination." But in those heady years, the '30s through the '50s and on into the '60s, the studio chiefs would dictate without fear of disobedience what should be done to alter a contract player's appearance. His (they were all men) taste would determine if an actress's hairline should be electrolytically shaped into a widow's peak, if a star should be put on amphetamines to lose baby fat, or if someone's nose needed reshaping because it looked too "ethnic." Thankfully this dictatorial practice has gone by the wayside, but there are still dozens of performers who find themselves having to change some features in order to make a good screen test.

The Hollywood beautifying industry has thus grown along with the entertainment industry, and the stars are their mutual productions. Besides plastic surgery, most famous movie stars have benefited from or at least been changed by the following:

1. Dental wizardry: orthodontia, capped teeth, bonding, and whitening.
2. Hair magic: cutting, styling, coloring, straightening, curling, extensions, toupees, and more.
3. Skin care: fighting acne, reducing wrinkles, age spots and pores, plumping up with Restylane or other fillers, nonablative laser treatments, hair removal.
4. Makeup artistry; smoothing, concealing, highlighting, enhancing, outlining.
5. Physical training: personal trainers, dietitians, massage, weights, machines, Pilates, Feldenkrais, yoga, Tai Bo, martial arts.
6. Wardrobe: stylists, unending designer discounts and freebies, and serious jewelry (usually loaned).

7.   Lighting: an underrated and incredibly sophisticated form of artistry, perhaps reaching its pinnacle in the black-and-white *film noir* of the '40s.

8.   Cinematography: the genius of painting with a camera.

9.   Perhaps the most effective secret of irresistibility is *real talent*. Beauty that comes from the inside is difficult to fake or to disguise.

In short, if you start with an already attractive individual, and then add all of the above, you wind up with an iconic ideal, a goal that is virtually unattainable for the normal, un-celebrity public. Unfortunately, in trying to attain that, many patients come up short, dissatisfied, and even more insecure than they were before they began.

Still, everyone wants to know: have these, our cherished celebrities, had plastic surgery or other cosmetic enhancement? The answer is *yes, they have*. It might have been a bit of Restylane or Botox injections, or it might have been a more invasive surgical procedure. Think of it this way: if a person is unbelievably beautiful, don't believe that they came by it entirely naturally. If a nose, a bosom, a face, lips, eyelids, or a figure looks "too good to be true," *it is*. Take this at face value, and don't knock yourself if you feel you don't measure up: *nobody's that perfect.*

CHAPTER THREE
BEVERLY HILLS HOUSE CALLS

An unwritten privilege that goes along with the mantle of celebrity is that of house calls or movie set calls or other location calls. They are not necessarily a remnant of country doctors in bygone eras. I have made many of them in my practice, often behind electric gates, sometimes surrounded by armed bodyguards.

Most of my celebrity patients don't really mind coming into the office before surgery or weeks later when they look fine. But during the healing stages, they really need to hide their famous faces from the curious public or the long lenses of the tabloid press photographers. They deserve their privacy under these circumstances.

I know that naming some of the following individuals would make these stories much more interesting, but revealing such confidences would not only be illegal, an inexcusable violation of ethics, and a very mean-spirited gesture, but it would also be the end of my practice. Moreover, the purpose of this book—if there actually is one—is *not* to just run through a list of famous people I've known. Rather I hope to show you, by means of these examples, the *human* side of my experiences with them and their influence on my own life. Despite their fame, they are only human, and never more so than when dealing with their doctors.

I've already mentioned Marilyn, who was not my patient. In fact, she died just when I was entering medical school. The other stories I can only relate by disguising the identities of the characters. I hope the impact is not lost in the translation. You may guess if you like. You'll probably be wrong, but there's no harm in trying. That said, I will start with a complete giveaway, graciously sanctioned by his widow, Kathy Brynner.

❖ *The King and I*

I was once called to the dressing room of the magnificent actor Yul Brynner when I had barely begun my practice. He had been referred to me by his internist, my neighbor in the medical building down the hall. He was my first celebrity patient, and he remains to this day the most charismatically elegant.

The reason he wanted to see a plastic surgeon (me) was not what most people would expect of such a famous actor in Beverly Hills. His concern was only a lipoma, a benign fatty tumor that had been gradually growing under the skin of his upper abdomen just below the ribs. At that time he was on stage virtually every night, strutting manfully around in his iconic role as the bare-chested King of Siam. The lipoma cast an odd-looking shadow on his abdomen from the overhead stage lights.

A lipoma? Not a face-lift? (Where would I hide the scars with that shaved head anyway?) And not even eyelids? Nothing of any significance from a plastic surgical point of view. A mere lipoma, the intern's delight, a piece of cake for a first-year resident. But a lipoma in a star of this magnitude was equivalent to a much larger procedure in a mere mortal. And I had been in practice in Beverly Hills for only about six months; I wasn't exactly a household name in the industry. Therefore, I approached the situation with awe and curiosity.

I had my worries. What if the wound didn't heal well? What if there was an infection? He had only one week before he was starting another long run of *The King and I*. If he couldn't go on stage because of a hideous scar, would they cancel the show? And what of all those people who had purchased seats already? How many hundreds of thousands of dollars would the producers stand to lose? Did he even have an understudy? He was the freakin' *King of Siam*! I was more anxious about this little lipoma than I had been since I was my a green-around-the-gills medical student and the resident handed me a scalpel, pointed at a boil on a patient's buttock, and said quietly, "Go ahead."

The tumor was easily removed, and the scar was barely perceptible. Yul Brynner was my patient and soon became my friend. I went to see *The King and I* many times, and always misted up at the sad ending. And each time, he would invite me back to his dressing room after the show. As with everything Yul did, it was always in the best of taste. At the first or second curtain call, a man would appear quietly by my seat and whisper, "Dr. Leaf, would you kindly come with me?" He would lead me backstage to the dressing room. I have been in many dressing rooms since, but Yul's dressing rooms were the only ones painted dark brown, at his request. A bottle of chilled Dom Perignon was always ready to be popped open, and the conversation was spirited, intelligent, and rarely about himself (a true anomaly among performers).

I have heard that in his professional life, he could be a bit difficult. Most truly great artists have that trait. I knew him only as a dazzling performer and a kind and worldly man. Even in his death from smoking-induced lung cancer, he performed an act of selflessness. He had taped a public service announcement warning us all of the dangers of smoking, only to be aired after his passing—a most effective visual memoir from a man who will long be remembered.

❖ *The Ocean's Roar*

In the mid-'80s, I did an abdominoplasty (tummy tuck) on a well-known actress who had had several babies and quite a few abdominal surgeries. Her abdomen was a patchwork of scars and loose skin, and I set about to repair the damage.

A typical abdominoplasty involves the removal of the skin and underlying fatty tissue between the belly button and the pubic area, where most of the damage has been done. The umbilicus (belly button) remains attached to the underlying abdominal muscles, and the tissue above the umbilicus is elevated to permit tightening of the muscles from the rib cage down to the pubis. The remaining flap of skin and fat is then pulled down tightly and stitched to the pubic area skin, and a hole in the flap is made for the umbilicus to come through. It is a somewhat invasive procedure and, at that time, was performed only in the hospital. Nowadays, this is done easily in the outpatient surgicenter.

As usual, my nurse reached into the "bag of names" and came up with an alias (probably Joan Newman again) for her admission to Midway Hospital. In those days, Cedars of Lebanon Hospital was where the stars went when they were pregnant, sick, or dying. When it came to plastic surgery, Midway was the obvious choice. It was smaller, quieter, and more private, and it was easier for people to remain incognito.

Actors are trained to be sensitive to their feelings and express their emotions openly. I clearly remember the moment when I removed the silicone rubber drain from her abdomen. This typically is not the most pleasant time, but it's not really painful, either. I gently tugged on the drain, and as it came out of the little wound, it must have given her a surprising jolt of pain.

Her scream still reverberates in my head. Nurses and technicians from the surrounding floors came running into her room, one of them pushing the crash cart.

After few days in the hospital, I discharged "Joan Newman" to her home for recuperation. Because she was living in Malibu and it would have been difficult for her to come into Beverly Hills for suture removal, I offered to come to her home.

Even though I had grown up in Chicago very close to Lake Michigan and had misspent most of the summer days of my youth at the beach, I hadn't had much leisure time to enjoy the incredible beaches of Southern California. I had been living in the San Fernando Valley and practicing in Beverly Hills, and a drive out to Malibu on a sunny Saturday afternoon was more of an opportunity than a chore. I brought along some instruments in my old doctor bag, the same bag that had been given to every freshman medical student in the country by Eli Lilly and Company. Courting of doctors by drug firms starts early.

Pacific Coast Highway was noisy and crowded as usual on a summer weekend. Traffic was snarled with noisy Harleys, "woodies," and sports cars with surfboards sticking out the open tops. The beach houses seemed very crowded together when viewed from their entries facing PCH, but their living areas looked out upon the ocean, which created an immediate sense of openness. Turning left across traffic to enter the driveway took some patience, but once I parked the car and entered the house, all became quiet and idyllic. I was stepping into another world.

Her bedroom had a wall of sliding glass doors overlooking the sand and surf. It had been two weeks since her surgery, and her sutures were ready to be removed. She was a little anxious about the pain of suture removal, but I reassured her that it would be pretty comfortable. The scream from ten days previously was a very fresh memory for me, and I was cautious to avoid another incident that would cause pain to her or to my eardrums.

She lay down on her bed, and I removed the dressing from her lower abdomen. I took out my forceps and scissors and began carefully to remove the stitches, working in controlled slow motion. I was intently focused, concentrating on being as gentle as possible when there was a *sudden crashing roar.* I jumped up, dropping my forceps and scissors on the floor.

"What the hell was *that?*" I said.

She looked up at me with her famous, movie star face and started laughing uncontrollably, holding her tummy to prevent it from hurting. Tears were streaming down her cheeks.

"You don't get down to the beach very often, do you?" she said, struggling to regain her breath.

My focus had been shattered by the crash of a wave on the shore. This phenomenon seemed to occur with regular frequency, an observation I humbly noted as I gathered up my instruments and what was left of my tattered professional demeanor.

We definitely didn't have waves like that in Chicago.

❖   *It's Okay. I'm a Doctor.*

She was one of the reigning sex bombs of the silver screen—red-haired, long-legged, voluptuous, and incredibly beautiful. She also had an unsettlingly sweet demeanor. I was usually rendered speechless every time I dealt with her, relying on my medical training to help me come up with a requisite amount of professional-sounding questions and profundities. I admit it—I am almost useless in the face of dazzling beauty.

I had done some liposuction on her already incredible body, and she asked me very sweetly if I wouldn't mind coming up to her house to take out the sutures. I agreed with the most professional detachment I could muster, and I drove up to her house. She had warned me that the tabloid press frequently camped outside her gates, so I needed to keep my windows up and make sure not speak to anyone outside. I rang the bell and identified myself as discreetly as possible, and the iron gates opened. I drove into the immense driveway, parked, and entered the house.

I was greeted by Mack, her houseman/bodyguard, a tight-bodied, handsome black dude. Although he greeted me with a smile and a handshake, I knew that he was capable of killing me with one hand and his eyes closed. He walked like a prowling cat as I followed him into her bedroom. She greeted me in her pink terry cloth robe, looking ravishing, and suggested to Mack that he wait outside. He closed the door behind him. I imagined a warning growl as he left.

The bedroom was furnished in "sex goddess moderne"—white carpet, white furniture, gold fixtures, and a huge circular bed beneath a mirrored ceiling. Honestly. I began to perspire lightly, and I was looking around for a suitable location to remove her sutures when she spoke from behind me.

"Right here on the bed should be fine." she said. I turned around, and she was already on the bed, completely naked.

"Is the light all right?" she asked charmingly.

"It's fine," I croaked. I busied myself getting my suture scissors and forceps ready and then began.

Liposuction is by and large a simple operation and leaves only very small scars and few sutures. In men, the most common areas of treatment are the "love handles" and the abdomen. In women, the usual areas treated are the outer thighs (saddlebags), the inner thighs, the lower tummy, the flanks, and sometimes the inner knees ... the Blue Plate Special.

My patient, although she was in great shape, had this typical combination of fat deposits, on a very conservative scale. The small stab incisions are hidden in creases here and there, such as the fold immediately below the buttock, the groin crease adjacent to the pubic areas, and the belly button. All are areas normally hidden from view, and most are areas considered rather private.

During the operation, the sterile setting of the operating room and the presence of the nurses and anesthetist helped create an air of professional detachment, but this was very different. There I was in the boudoir of boudoirs, on my knees, with my ravishingly beautiful patient rolling into different positions to make it easier for me.

I consciously fought the impulse, but I couldn't help stealing a glance at the mirror on the ceiling above, at which point an odd thought came into my head: "What would my professors at the University of Chicago think of me now?" This was definitely not research in molecular biology. Even worse, I was certain that at any second the door to the bedroom would burst open and Mack would be upon me with a flying kick of instant decapitation.

I had no need for concern. My patient was very accustomed to being naked in front of strangers. Not until about twenty years had passed did I figured out that she was actually having fun with me, enjoying watching the sweat on the brow of this very un-Hollywood doctor so obviously from the Midwest. Years later, she admitted that truth to me, and we laughed together at the memory.

She healed very well, and she has continued to be my patient for other procedures. The only difference is that now she comes *to the office* for suture removal.

The light is better.

❖   *A Desperate Diva*

One Saturday morning, I was in the kitchen toasting a bagel when the answering service called with an urgent message from a patient of mine, a star in the world of song and dance. She had been busy for weeks rehearsing a new dance routine for her Las Vegas revue opening that evening. She had gotten a manicure earlier that morning and, while practicing a pirouette, somehow managed to slice into the skin of her nose with *her own extra sharp fingernail.*

It's typical of cuts on the face that they bleed rather profusely, and because she had been on regular aspirin doses, the bleeding was even more impressive. This is the reason patients should stop taking aspirin a full two weeks before any elective surgery in order to prevent bleeding complications.

Her manager had a cool head and managed to stop the bleeding with some ice and pressure, but she was distraught.

Would she be able to make her performance that evening?

Would she need stitches?

Would it leave a scar?

Could I come over right away and take care of it?

Come over right away? She was in her hotel on the Las Vegas Strip, and I was at home in my kitchen, in another state, in my bathrobe, toasting a bagel. I looked at Judy for wifely advice, and we both agreed that a night in Vegas could be fun, so I told my distraught diva that I'd be on the next flight and that I'd see her soon.

We quickly packed an overnight bag. This was well before 9/11, so I was able to carry some instruments directly on the plane. We hopped a flight at Burbank airport, and within two hours we were at her hotel on the Strip.

She had regained her composure by the time I arrived. I removed the Band-Aid and checked the wound on the bridge of her nose. As I expected, the wound was very tiny, somewhat like a small paper cut. Although I came prepared with instruments and sutures, I also brought Steri-Strips (tape strips) and some sticky solution on the hunch that there was more smoke than fire in this scenario.

In about five minutes, I had cleansed the skin and the cut and applied the sticky solution and the Steri-Strip, and all was well with the world. Despite the miniscule nature of the injury, she was enormously relieved by my presence and the little bit of care that I had tendered—such is the temperament of a diva. She even could put her makeup right over the tape, and no one had a clue at her performance that anything odd had happened. The show must go on, and it did. Plus, Judy and I had fantastic seats without having to bribe the seating host.

❖   *Kitchen Table Surgery*

This might be more correctly referred to as a *reverse* house call. Mrs. Z is one of the reigning queens of the soaps. I personally wasn't into the daytime dramas, mainly because I was usually working during the day. Nonetheless, these actors were recognized and idolized by millions of fans, not only in the States but in Europe as well.

I have discovered that daytime stars tend to be more "normal" than their counterparts in prime-time TV and films. They work almost on a nine-to-five basis, and if they are lucky, they work almost daily, without breaks, for the better part of the year. They have a job to do. They're happy to have the work, and they work very hard. They may be viewed with mild disdain by the more highly paid movie stars or by the more serious Broadway actors, but they have a regular gig. Pecking order aside, it's a great living.

Mrs. Z has two small children: one of them fell off his bicycle on a Sunday morning, and she called me in a panic. Could she bring him over to the house? She lived a short distance from me, and before I could say okay, they were at my doorstep. Her five-year-old son carried a small plastic bag with crushed ice cubes pressed up against his chin. I picked him up and placed him on the kitchen table, which was just the right height and had good lighting, and coaxed him into letting me look at his "owie." There was a small cut, about a half an inch long, just under the chin.

I do many face-lifts, and I usually make a small incision right under the chin in order to work on the neck fat and muscles. Interestingly enough, I often find a little scar in that area from just such an injury as I was now facing. In fact, I would estimate that as many as one-third of the people in the world have a scar in that position.

Once again, I reached into my old doctor bag, and with young Master Z lying on the kitchen table, his mother holding him gently but firmly, I injected a small amount of local anesthetic into the wound. (Interesting note: inserting a needle through the cut edges of a wound instead of through intact skin doesn't hurt.) A few small sutures later and he was back together and running out the door. He came to my office for suture removal a few days later, and at that time, he was a little confused about why he had to sit in an exam chair instead of my kitchen table.

❖ *Il Dottore and the Red Knee*

For about a decade, I accompanied my wife on biannual trips to Milan to assist her with the buying for the Beverly Hills Prada boutique, which, to my everlasting amazement, we owned. (That's another story.) Judy was the boss, the main buyer, and stylist. I was her assistant buyer and presumably the business person. This was absurd, of course. Everyone knows that doctors, like artists, have the worst business heads imaginable. Somehow, we just got very lucky, and even my inadequacies in that realm couldn't ruin it. I do, however, have a much greater respect for successful businesspeople as a result of my efforts.

Other than my experience with preppy college men's clothing, I knew very little about the world of fashion. However, a few years of on-the-job training gave me more knowledge of fashion than I ever could imagine or desire. Sitting in a vast room surrounded by thousands of handbags or dresses or suits or shoes, selecting colors, fabrics, and sizes, watching enormous budgets being met and exceeded, I found that there was much more to the world than plastic surgery. I learned the difference between a regular clutch and *menaudiere*, between a T-strap and a sling-back pump, between a straight skirt and a pleated one, between a bag or shoe made of *pressed* (said with air of disdain) skin or one made of a genuine hide.

I found myself becoming involved in a completely new universe. We grew to know and become friends with many remarkably talented people whom I never would have met in the medical world or in the narrow confines of Beverly Hills. Although some of them knew that

I was a plastic surgeon, to most I was merely Judy Leaf's husband and assistant buyer, another *garmento*. There were, however, a few exceptions.

A very successful model was a patient and friend of mine. She was always at the collections in Milan whenever we were there, working the various designers' runways. Once or twice a year she was in Los Angeles and came in for her wrinkle fillers or Botox injections.

I was preparing to leave for Milan at the end of February for the fall-winter collection when Miss L called me and asked if I could bring some collagen (the filler of choice in those days) with me to inject her wrinkles. I was leery of doing so, because the product needed to be refrigerated and because I was uncertain of the legality of the situation. I had nothing remotely like an Italian medical license, and I didn't want to run into trouble with the *Carabinieri*. She reassured me that it would be completely confidential, and because she was already a patient of mine, there would be no cause for concern.

I went out and bought a little insulated carrier meant for medications like insulin, filled it with collagen syringes and a Botox vial, and made the trip as planned. Miss L got her lips and frown lines injected in our room at the Four Seasons, and then we all went down to the lobby for drinks. We joined a group of her model friends, and she confessed to them what I had done. Immediately, they all wanted collagen, Botox, whatever I could offer. Fortunately (or unfortunately), I hadn't brought any more than I needed for L, and I was able to beg off. At that point, one of the girls, a superstar among models, asked me to look at her knee, which was giving her some trouble.

The Four Seasons Hotel on Via Gesu is the epicenter of fashion week in Milan. The lobby filled up with buyers, models, publicists, and various hangers-on starting around 7:00 PM. The Russian pianist was working the temperament of the room, alternating between Rachmaninoff and Lara's Theme. Each season, on one particular night, the lobby rapidly and quietly emptied as the models and others moved down the street en masse to the Versace palazzo for the first of the two shows.

Gianni Versace was at the height of his fame at that time, and his fashion show was one of the most coveted tickets. One hour later, the lobby filled up again, bubbling over with conversation in an excited but typically muted Milanese fashion. The models returned in their bathrobes, hair in curlers, taking up one or two seating areas, drinks in hand. Then one hour later, all quieted down again as the second show of the evening commenced.

Mme Red Knee consulted me just before the first show of that evening. She had a question about one of her remarkable-looking legs. I suggested discreetly leaving the crowded lobby for a more private consultation, but she hiked up her skirt and placed her leg squarely on my lap. Models have no fear of the public display of skin. If they did, they wouldn't work very much.

I looked hastily around the room, but no one seemed to be taking notice of the fact that one of the world's top models was placing her leg on my lap. I also glanced at my wife, who showed no signs of seething. When I focused my attention on the knee, I was alarmed. She had a large area of redness around the kneecap, and it was tender to the touch. Redness extended up her leg, which was a dangerous sign.

I felt that she could very well have a septic joint, an infection in the knee joint itself, with perhaps an early lymphangitic spread of the infection into the lymph glands. This was a potentially serious situation. In the States, I would have recommended hospitalization, bed rest, and strong intravenous antibiotics. I suggested we ask the concierge for referral to a local doctor, but RK said that there was no way she would do that, she had to do these two Versace shows and leave for the *Prêt à Porter* in Paris the next day. Couldn't she just take some antibiotic pills?

This was a dilemma: I had been trained for many years not to compromise on what I knew to be the best medical course of action, but here I was in Milan. I knew no orthopedists. I spoke only menu Italian, and this was a very fabulous knee indeed. I was way out of my customary medical milieu. I gave her some broad-spectrum antibiotics of my own after I extracted a promise from her that she would see the local orthopedic doctor in Paris the next day.

She did the show, flew to Paris the following day, and saw her doctor. Apparently, everything worked out just fine. Both of her legs, along with the rest of her, were signed for a major hosiery campaign a month later.

As one of my professors always reminded me, "It's better to be a lucky surgeon than a good surgeon."

❖ *A Genuine Beverly Hills Princess*

Like most Americans, I'm not really comfy with actual European-style royalty. We have our icons, our screen idols, and our elected politicians. Penetrating the aura of celebrity that surrounds them is tough enough, but dealing face-to-face with royalty can be an exercise in awkwardness. Do I say, "Your Highness," "Your Lordship," or "Your Grace"? Does anyone really care? After thirty years of practice and many encounters with blue bloods from various parts of the world, I'm still a little uneasy dealing with them. Of course, from a surgeon's point of view, blood is always red, or at least it ought to be.

I usually ask, so as not to appear like a bumpkin, "How would you prefer I address you?" The patient may offer their first name, in which case I offer mine. Once that is out of the way, the patient is the patient. Pretense and attitude are relaxed, and there is a feeling of a "normal" doctor-patient relationship that develops. They may be a bit more worldly and more accustomed to privilege than the average patient, but they have the same anxieties about their medical care as anyone else.

There was one amusing exception to this rule. Princess R was a prominent member of a royal family from an oil-rich country in the Middle East. She was no "normal" patient. Many royals from Europe have title and heritage but no real wealth, but the princess had it all. And when I asked how she would prefer to be addressed, she replied with a slightly raised eyebrow, "Princess R" of course. That settled that.

Besides her enormous wealth, she also had had *way* too much plastic surgery (see *"When Is Too Much Not Enough?"*), but she seemed quite pleased with her appearance. She sought my consultation because her breasts, which had been augmented several years previously, had become hard and deformed.

Breast implants are always soft to begin with. In fact, the implant itself never changes its character. The hardness and deformity that may appear in the breast are the result of the scar "capsule" which surrounds it. (See *Are Those Real?*)

The only semi-reliable means of softening the breast is by surgically removing the capsule, replacing the implant with a new one, and hoping that the problem doesn't recur. It usually works. Much progress has been made in prevention of this capsular contracture, but it still occurs often enough to remain the most common problem associated with breast implants of any type.

The princess arrived in my office with a large retinue. There were the usual two women-servants, fluttering around her like little birds, attending to her unspoken commands instantly and enthusiastically. There were also two somber, hawkeyed bodyguards lurking around, acting as if an assassin were about to spring from my recovery room. And there was her driver, a mountain of a man, sitting quietly at the wheel of her illegally parked, armored Mercedes limo, a Middle Eastern *Odd-Job*.

The princess spoke flawless British-toned English, and she surrounded herself with an aura of world-weary imperiousness. I politely ushered her group out of the examination room—except for one of her attendants and my nurse—and then proceeded to examine her royal breasts. They were as hard as rocks, grade four out of a possible four. They couldn't have been any harder. She concurred with a nod.

I recommended removal of the implants and scar capsule and replacement with newer implants of a design that would greatly reduce the chance of recurrence (the *Meme* implant, a silicone gel implant coated with a polyurethane foam, which is, sadly, no longer available). I also offered to do her follow-up examination and suture removal in her own home to ensure confidentiality. In her case, it was more to avoid overcrowding my waiting room with scowling security personnel.

The operation proceeded as planned several weeks later, and everything ran smoothly. The scar capsules were unusually hard, thick, and calcific, like eggshell. At the finish of the operation, her breasts were smooth and soft. Dressings were applied, and she was moved to the recovery room. Two hours later, she was discharged in the care of a nurse to her home.

The next day, I made the first of many house calls. I soon became accustomed to the gate with intercom and video surveillance, the long winding driveway leading to the parking area filled with German cars and Uzi-brandishing guards in white polo shirts with black slacks. I kept reminding myself that I was still in America—and in Beverly Hills to boot.

The house itself was a Marrakesh/Palm Springs palace, and I was ushered in quickly. My eyes immediately took in the white walls, white carpet, white domed ceilings, and white furniture. To be more precise, the carpet was once white. There were dogs everywhere: barking big dogs, yipping little dogs, and puppies in a big temporary corral in the center of the living room. The resulting din almost overwhelmed the other competing sounds—bird sounds.

In the rooms where the dogs were not allowed, a multitude of birds squawked and cackled, and some warbled. A few were in ornate cages, but most had the run of the house, and flew to the chandeliers and the tops of the potted palms. They seemed to enjoy taunting the dogs, especially the puppies, by flying very close and flapping their wings at the little ones' noses. Not surprisingly, there was an enormous amount of bird excrement and dog urine stains everywhere. There seemed to be enough servants to keep ahead of the dog excrement, but the bird poop was something else.

The dining room was dominated by a huge table made from a single enormous slab of beautiful green malachite. I think it was malachite, but I wasn't certain because of the large quantity of hardened mini-stalactites of bird shit encrusting it. Someone explained that the person whose job it was to scrape this clean was away on holiday. *A well-deserved holiday,* I thought to myself.

Some of the larger and more aggressive dogs had to be restrained so I could cross the room and enter the bedroom. The princess apparently had a deep love for animals but not a great deal of concern about pet excrement. On the other hand, she was scrupulously clean in her personal habits. She had her nurse accompany me to the bathroom to observe me while I washed my hands, and then, surrounded by a host of luxurious Porthault guest towels, I was given a roll of paper toweling to dry my hands. I was clearly the hired help here.

Her postoperative course was quite routine, and she recovered well and was pleased with her results. At least I assume that she was. She never acknowledged her satisfaction verbally, but she returned a few years later for a secondary face-lift. The most sincere compliments are often unspoken, a subtle nod from a royal to a humble doctor.

❖   *Capri*

At the end of a winding path on the Isle of Capri stands a monument carved by the wind. The Arco Naturale, or Natural Arch, is a jagged narrow bridge of granite that frames a serene view of the Tyrrhenian Sea lapping at the rocky shore several hundred meters below. I have decided that when I die, I want my ashes to be scattered through it. (My Virgo brain annoyingly reminds me of the persistent updraft which would blow the ashes back in the face of the scatterers—what to do?)

Nearby, a zigzag footpath provides a route down the cliff's side to my favorite restaurant on the island, and perhaps in the world. Fontelina Beach Club and Restaurant sits on the rocky shore. There is no beach.

The day is spent in a lethargic, pleasant haze. You lie on mats and towels or sit on little wooden beach chairs under umbrellas stuck in holes in the rock slabs. You enter the water by diving off the rocks. Mostly, you drink the delicious freshly made sangria and read the *Herald Tribune,* swimming only enough to cool off from the hot Italian sun. You also try not to stare at the beautiful young topless sunbathers, chatting away in Italian and smoking cigarettes in the most charming manner.

The restaurant itself is an open-air, thatched-roof affair with tables overlooking the sea and the crowd of exotic motor yachts moored nearby. And the food is simply the best—Neapolitan cooking at its simplest and most appealing. How much can you say about bufala mozzarella so fresh it was still in the bufala only yesterday and so firm that it squeaks when you cut it? About tomatoes sweet and fresh straight from the vine? Homemade pasta, freshly caught fish, and for dessert, the famous Caprese Torte with an espresso?

But wait … I'm not a food critic, I'm a plastic surgeon, and I'm merely trying to set the scene for the encounter. Capri does stimulate one's sensory memories.

One sunny August afternoon, after lunch with my family and friends, I was slowly making my way along the rock slabs toward our umbrellas when a tall, slender bronzed woman approached me somewhat tentatively and said "Hello."

She was beautiful—long blond hair pulled back with an Hermes scarf, mirrored Chanel sunglasses, white linen tunic over leopard bikini, sandals with gold leather thongs, and a great deal of gold and diamond jewelry everywhere.

I looked behind me to see whom she was addressing.

"Dr. Leaf, don't you remember me?" she breathed, with a sultry Italian accent. "You saved my life!"

She removed her wraparound sunglasses, and I recognized her.

I had first met her at the bar in the Hotel Danieli in Venice several winters earlier. (I know, this sounds like a *film noir* opening.) She had called my office from Venice while I was on a skiing vacation in Northern Italy with my family. She was extremely agitated and most eager to have a consultation with me. I had recently operated on a socially important friend of hers from Rome, and she had given her my name.

My secretary mentioned that coincidentally I would also be in Venice tomorrow, staying at the Danieli Hotel. Before the day was out, the meeting had been set up. I was to meet her in the bar at 5:00 PM the next day.

The Danieli is a fourteenth-century palazzo, whose ornate décor defines rococo. The lobby has multicolored marble columns reaching up two stories to the frescoed ceiling. Hanging from the ancient scalloped beams are huge chandeliers made of red Murano glass with gilt trim.

I went to the bar a few minutes early and asked the host for a small table in the back of the room and then I waited by the front entrance. Outside, it was dark and raining with a cold wind blowing off the Grand Canal, a typical Venetian January.

She swept into the lobby like a grand duchess, her floor-length black raincoat and her long mane of streaked blond hair flying, striding powerfully in high leather boots, a crocodile bag over her shoulder. She was magnificent—a traffic stopper. She introduced herself to me in excellent English, and we walked into the bar. The host looked up from his desk at me and smiled. He then looked at her and snapped to attention as he welcomed her.

"*Buona Sera, Senora!*" He bowed and escorted us to the first booth in the very front of the room. He glanced back at me with a subtle raised eyebrow. It was immediately clear that I risen a few pegs in his esteem.

We sat down, and I helped her take off her raincoat. It was completely lined with Russian sable. We ordered tea, and began to talk.

Within a very few minutes, she had explained to me that her husband had taken a mistress. I avoided commenting that most Americans thought this was business as usual in Italy. She was bereft, and she began to tear up. She feared her marriage was over. She hoped that I could help her by making her look more youthful so that her husband would want her again.

She soon regained control, and I looked at her more closely. She was quite beautiful, in her late forties I guessed, with only a slight amount of looseness around her jowls and neck and some excess skin in the upper lids. But in that light, with her makeup on, in the front of the now-crowded room, it would be difficult to do a proper evaluation. Besides, I needed to touch her face and thought that might look odd in that setting.

She suggested we go up to my room.

This is Italy, I thought to myself, but I didn't feel that my hotel room would be an appropriate venue for a clinical examination. Besides, my wife was due back at any minute, and there would have to be a lot of explaining.

I suggested we go out into a portion of the lobby that was somewhat secluded but brightly lit, and there I was able to feel her face and determine the degree of tissue laxity. I suggested that I could probably give her enough improvement to make it worth her while, but I repeated several times that there was absolutely no way I could even hint to her that having a face-lift would save her marriage. In fact, I advised her quite bluntly that it rarely makes a difference in a situation like this. She said that she had definitely decided to have the surgery anyway and would make an appointment to come to Beverly Hills the next month.

She did. She had her face-lift and upper blepharoplasty (eyelid repair), recovered very nicely, and went home after about ten days. I didn't hear from her again—until three and a half years later when she materialized on the rocky path by the restaurant, repeating over and over that I had saved her life. After a brief discussion, I discerned that her marriage was intact, that her husband had dismissed the mistress with a handshake and a handsome check, and that she was still blissfully in love with her once-errant spouse, who was standing patiently by as we spoke.

Somewhere around the eighth or ninth "you saved my life," my wife started tugging at my shirtsleeve.

"Get me out of here," she muttered.

I was hesitant. La Senora had just finished inviting me and my family to join them on their beautiful yacht anchored enticingly offshore. This was a dilemma of serious proportions.

Propriety and recognition of how uncomfortable my wife was becoming helped me make my decision. I graciously thanked la Senora and her husband and we returned to our shady little nest on the rocks.

❖ *Beware the Jet Lag*

Andre Miripolski is an artist with an abiding sense of joy, which he expresses in riotous semiabstract cartoonlike creations. Today, he is a good friend and a prolific painter/sculptor, but there was a time when he very nearly lost his life.

We met at a wonderful party, a wedding of mutual friends in an ancient fortress town in southern France. It was an extraordinary event. I don't think I've ever had more scrumptious food, but the party after the dinner was really a one-off. We all had been instructed to dress in either black tie or medieval garb. Sartorial compromiser that I am, I wore a tux with a very old bow tie. And when the feast was over around midnight, we all returned to our rooms to change for the after party. I really wanted to go to bed and watch CNN, but the romance of the evening carried me along—bountiful champagne, great live Brazilian music, and dancing. Bedtime was at sunrise, and no one slept, for fear of missing an exceptional breakfast.

Before and during the wedding, I got to know Andre. He was a smiling, upbeat, colorful man in his early thirties, and we became good friends instantly. He had an insatiable curiosity about plastic surgery, seeing it very much as another art form. I was flattered and happy to find that we could discuss concepts of art and beauty in a manner I found comfortable. Andre made everyone feel comfortable.

We all went our separate ways the next day, and my wife and I returned home. Two weeks later, Andre arrived home. He was driving his small Renault on the San Diego Freeway the day after his arrival when jet lag overcame him. He fell asleep at the wheel, crashed into the center divider, and the car flipped over several times before coming to a halt. He was taken, unconscious and severely injured, to the UCLA emergency room, where he was promptly admitted and taken to surgery.

Andre had broken just about everything breakable: both legs, both arms, and pelvis. Plus, he had ruptured his spleen. But his most life-threatening injuries were above the neck: skull fractures, concussions, and a Le Forte III fracture, where the bones of the face were literally broken away from the skull. He endured days of surgery, all emergency. Finally, after about two very difficult weeks, his condition had become stable enough that longer-term plans were being formed.

Artists do not necessarily live in the reality-based world that most of us inhabit. They don't really pay much attention to things like business and savings accounts, let alone insurance. Andre was completely uninsured.

At that time, as today, there were programs administered by the state and federal government to help pay for the care of indigent uninsured patients, but it would be necessary for Andre to be transferred to LA County Hospital. This was not necessarily a tragedy, because the hospital was (and is) an excellent trauma center.

Andre had gradually regained his senses and called me, managing to speak through clenched teeth, which had been wired together as part of his facial fracture repairs. I went to see him in the hospital. I had treated facial injuries of this magnitude before, but seeing a recently acquired friend so dramatically changed was a shock. There were steel wires protruding from his head which were attached to an external steel framework, a "halo" apparatus designed to hold the bony fragments in place until they healed. His teeth were wired together, and there were plaster casts and wires in his arms and hands and legs. He looked like a cartoon character version of an injured person.

But he was no cartoon. He was the same kind, gentle, and inexplicably joyous person I had met a few weeks earlier, nine time zones and a thousand years away from the steel wires, the cumbersome bandages, and the beeping monitors. And he enthusiastically proclaimed that this accident was to be an inspiration for his work.

Andre really did not want to be transferred, and it was very much in his favor to stay where he was. I was then (and am today) a member of the clinical faculty at UCLA, which means that I help to train the plastic surgery residents at the medical center. I hoped I would be able to intervene to some degree on his behalf. I had very limited clout when it came to the financial aspects of health care. I lobbied the departmental chief on Andre's behalf to see what could be done.

UCLA came to the rescue. There were certain research funds for the craniofacial section of the plastic surgery department, and these were made available for Andre's care. That, along with the state funds, provided enough for Andre to remain at UCLA as long as needed for several additional operations.

When he was finally discharged, Andre returned home. He set about to express his inspiration in his work. His home was an industrial loft space filled with large constructions, his usual type of work. During his convalescence, confined to a wheelchair, his arms and legs in casts, he had to rescale the scope of his work to that which he could handle on his wheelchair tray.

Andre created a series of small collages which told the story of his accident and his recovery. It was titled "Fear No Art: A Crash Course in Humanity." He expressed himself more eloquently in this manner than any narrative I have ever read. And he subsequently had a benefit showing, which raised funds for the research program in the division of plastic surgery at UCLA—his personal payback.

Although I've performed a few touch-ups on his face over the ensuing years, my part in Andre's treatment was small. Mostly, my input was as a friend and conduit to my skilled colleagues at UCLA, who put this kind and creative Humpty Dumpty back together again. Andre's face is still a little crooked, but his smile is as warm and honest as when I first met him at a very grand party in France.

❖   *Ship's Doctor*

Of all the places I have visited in the world, none makes me feel poorer or more anonymous than Monte Carlo. Its physical presence rises from the harbor in tiers of high-rise condos, each competing for the best view of the sea, as well as the best spot to be seen. Hotel de Paris sits at the base along the harbor's edge on a cul-de-sac that has at its end the famed casino. If you have ever watched the Monte Carlo Grand Prix on television, you've seen the race course passing the hotel on every lap.

A few years ago, I was there with my family on a chartered yacht. Arriving in Monte Carlo harbor by yacht is a great equalizer. Never mind that our boat could easily have served as the tender to some of the more extravagant queens of the sea; there is an egalitarian sense of camaraderie among yachting people that I was happy to assume for the ten days of our charter. It was definitely good to be king.

I had checked with my office that afternoon, and I was told that a Saudi businessman had called from Monte Carlo, requesting an appointment. He was told that, coincidentally, I would be in that very area that very same day. I was given a cell phone number to call upon arrival. A genteel Saudi man answered and asked if he and his wife could meet me later at the bar in the Hotel de Paris to discuss a plastic surgery issue. We agreed on 5:00 PM, which sounded like the time that James Bond would have requested his first shaken-not-stirred vodka martini.

At the appointed time, I walked into the bar, not feeling at all like James Bond. The bar was a large room with crystal chandeliers, many tables and chairs, and large picture windows overlooking the ocean. The women were typically older and more bejeweled than they were at other chic locations on the Riviera, and that day was no exception. Diamonds, emeralds, rubies, and sapphires were in abundance, and it was still only teatime.

Mr. and Mrs. A arrived shortly after I did. They were friendly and engaging, and had been educated in the United States. He was short, round, and much balder than I, and she was about the same but with more hair. He wanted me to examine his wife for a face-lift and liposuction. They had a friend who had been my patient, and they hoped I would take care of her as well.

The face examination was not a problem at that place, especially in the afternoon light, the distracting glint of diamonds notwithstanding. Evaluating her liposuction needs was another issue. Sexy young women might have been showing a lot of thigh in that room, but the mature and discreet Mrs. A presented a different situation. I asked if there was a place we could go to facilitate the examination.

"Of course," he replied. "Our boat is just outside in the harbor." I nodded. I had never done a physical examination on a yacht before. There was a first time for everything, I guessed.

The front door of the Hotel de Paris has more super-car power than any venue outside of the Geneva Auto Show. Ferarris, Lamborghinis, Bentleys were all lined up perfectly like soldiers, sunlight glinting off the polished chrome. We walked out the front door of the hotel into the hot August afternoon. A white Corniche convertible was waiting, driver/bodyguard at the wheel. I told Judy that if I wasn't back in an hour to call Interpol. I was only half kidding. The bodyguard looked serious.

Although Monte Carlo has a beautiful harbor where our charter was moored, many yachters keep their vessels in Fonteville harbor, which is about a ten-minute drive across the border into France. (I am told it has something to do with taxes.) We glided majestically through the city and arrived shortly at Fonteville.

We drove along the pier to the stern of a large yacht approximately forty meters (about 125 feet) in length. We walked the gangplank and entered the salon of the boat, with its plush white carpets, glass sculptures, and white wood trim. The décor was elegantly Middle Eastern. We descended to the master cabin, a large room with gold fixtures and a king-size bed with a white duvet. The air-conditioning was set to stun.

The bodyguard waited outside the door while I examined Mrs. A. She was a little portly. She had two grown children, and liposuction might remove some of the fullness of the thighs, but it was questionable whether or not she would perceive any improvement at all. She simply needed to lose some weight and work out a bit. I felt it my duty to recommend against the procedure, but I wanted to do it without offending my patient. It's always a narrow line to walk under any circumstances, but in this opulent, very foreign setting with someone who could have whatever she wanted, it was even more difficult. Surprisingly, her husband agreed with me. And in the Middle East, it seems, that's all that matters.

She did come to Beverly Hills that fall and had her face-lift. She healed very well and invited Judy and me to their annual Fourth of July party in Monte Carlo the following summer. It was a genuinely sweet invitation, but one that we politely declined. We usually like to celebrate Independence Day at home with our family in the traditional American way: barbecue, beer, fireworks-watching, and mosquito-swatting.

Maybe next year.

CHAPTER FOUR
ARE THOSE REAL?

One of the bright ideas to encourage people to get out of their cars and walk the streets in Southern California is the sidewalk café. They're popping up all over town like Santa Barbara shrimp on arugula. Even traditional restaurants and delis have joined the party, with outdoor eating areas ranging from a single table with two folding chairs serving frozen yogurt to fenced-off street-side full table service. Ten million Frenchmen can't be wrong after all. Outdoor dining on an active thoroughfare provides a constantly changing source of lively conversation.

In Paris, the conversations are animated, smoke-filled, political, and intense. In Beverly Hills, the conversers are apt to be more laid back, but the subject matter equally weighty: "Dude, is that a turbo?" or "Oh my god, what did she do to her face?" or the most pertinent of all, "Are those real?" Although the question might refer to earrings or designer handbags, it usually doesn't.

Sitting at an outdoor table at Cafe del Arte in my building, I observe that the world going by is predictable in its individuality. Men jump out of their Porsches wearing sneakers, expensive but worn-looking jeans, T-shirts, and baseball hats. Women of all ages try to appear young and sexy. The uniform for the young hottie is the following: tight scoop-neck sleeveless T-shirts, bare midriffs,

70

tight hip-hugging jeans, mules, Chanel sunglasses with blue lenses. For the hipper, more affluent studio exec wives, a different look prevails: jeans (of course), white T-shirt, Birkin bags, and Ugg boots or flip-flops. Nonconformity may have been the prod that got many to seek a new freedom in the West, but once here, they want to know the drill.

Because I am sitting on Bedford Drive ("the Street" in plastic surgery terms), yet another scene is manifest. There are so many doctors here, particularly plastic surgeons and their staffs, that one sees a lot of people in scrub suits—not necessarily the tried and true green but also beige, gray, blue, and plum, with white lab coats over them. One doctor walks around with black scrubs strategically cut off to show his biceps and triceps. Another ambles up and down in his scrubs, softly hitting a tennis ball with a polo mallet. There is also an alternative medicine clinic in my building, run by American Sikhs, so white turbans, coats, and wrapped-leg pants with sneakers are prevalent. Middle America is very, very far away.

There are teenagers with splints on their noses and bruised eyes, and women with bandages around their faces. Other medical disciplines are here, too, so you see young patients on crutches and old ones in wheelchairs with attendants and oxygen tanks trailing. There are gaunt chemotherapy patients, heavy obesity clinic patients, and anxious psychotherapy patients. And there are the paparazzi, lounging around like earthbound vultures looking for their next meal.

Still, the visual that commands the most attention, the most gawks and goofy grins is the tight tank top or T-shirt stretched out by a pair of enormous breasts. Even when I know they are implants— even when it's my own work—it's hard not to stare. I am a doctor, and I try to maintain an air of professionally detachment, but there is something about large breasts, real or not, that is mesmerizing to men (and women), straight or gay. Those who sport these huge appendages know that … and enjoy it.

It's not surprising that breast augmentation surgery is among the most popular plastic surgery procedures performed here and elsewhere. The female breast is connected in profound and powerful ways to our basic concept of femininity. In one instance maternal and nurturing, in another alluringly sexual, breasts have a universal importance, particularly in Western society.

And don't think that interest in the female breast is a twentieth-century, *Playboy*-induced phenomenon. A famous Paleolithic carving, unearthed in Willendorf, Germany, many years ago, is a small carved stone statue of a woman's torso, consisting largely of two full breasts and an equally impressive set of buttocks. Cavemen obviously had more on their minds than just hunting and gathering.

From the time-honored tradition of stuffing gym socks in a training bra to the current popularity of the Wonderbra and many similar devices, a woman's wish to make her breasts more alluring remains intimate and strong. And "alluring" may be a vastly different concept between women, and even for the same woman at different times in her life. A younger, thin woman with very small breasts may dream of being larger and more voluptuous, whereas a more mature, heavier woman may feel that larger breasts are matronly, and long for a smaller, upturned "perky" look. And a woman who has lost a breast to cancer may find herself with a precariously low sense of self-worth and feminine identity.

The female bosom is conspicuously displayed in virtually every advertisement directed at men, whether it's an ad for beer, automobiles, cigarettes, clothing, or restaurants. Simply put, *sex sells!* Perhaps the sexiest visual, particularly for the sixteen- to thirty-six-year-old male, is a "rack," a conspicuously displayed set of large breasts with a good amount of cleavage.

The constant presence of provocative images throughout our

popular culture tends to reinforce these desires, and the garment industry has responded by providing ingenious designs to enhance, conceal, amplify, or minimize the breasts, depending on the fashion of the times. Think of the openly voluptuous necklines emphasized by the high Empire waistlines of the court of Napoleon, and then think of the high-necked, small-waistline styles of Edwardian England— two extremes within one century and a hundred miles of each other, both of which emphasized the bosom.

Our intellects and technological abilities have advanced exponentially, but the breast remains a fundamentally sexy thing. Tastes in the particulars may have changed over the years, even in recent times. Witness the changes in brassieres. In the '50s bras were designed to "lift and separate." In the '60s, they were burned. In the '70s, they lifted and pushed together. Then came the Wonderbra, Curves, the water bra, and other contrivances meant to create the illusion of large, firm, full breasts. It is a small leap in execution and a major leap in perception to create breasts that maintain that illusion *without* bras. Often that's the goal of breast augmentation and the reason for its popularity.

❖   *The False Start*

If you are familiar with the '60s, you may remember Carol Doda. She was an exotic dancer at the Condor, one of the more established topless bars in the North Beach section of San Francisco. "Exotic dancer" was, of course, a euphemism for "stripper." In the late '60s during the summer of love, the Haight-Ashbury area was the center for the Flower Power movement—acid rock, psychedelic clothes, hippies, and antiwar protesters flourished. Drugs were everywhere, and many taboos came crashing down. Exotic dancers became strippers. Call girls became hookers. And breasts became huge.

Carol Doda achieved her fame not because of her skill with a brass pole but because of the enormity of her breasts. She was featured in

Playboy, made the talk show rounds, and became a household name—at least in fraternity houses. If her breasts were the most striking thing about her, how they got that way was even more shocking. Her breasts had been enlarged to gigantic proportions by means of silicone injections. *Not implants, but injections of liquid silicone.*

Although Dr. Cronin and Dr. Gerow had just published their pioneering work on silicone breast implants in 1962 in Houston, Texas, an underground cottage industry in silicone injections was already thriving. Liquid silicone had been the subject of some interesting research papers, showing promise in correcting contour deformities of the face. But at that time, absolutely no research had been conducted on the safety of the product, particularly when injected into the breast, an organ which in its unaltered state can become cancerous in 7–8 percent of women.

But it was so easy. A doctor, usually of dubious credentials, could buy industrial-grade silicone by the drum or medical-grade silicone by the liter. Some practitioners would use a formula of industrial-grade silicone *laced with cobra venom*, which would create inflammation and subsequent scar tissue to keep the liquid in place. The only instruments needed were a hypodermic syringe and a fairly large needle. Come into the office and leave with breasts one or two cup sizes larger fifteen minutes later. Come back next week and go for three or four. No surgery, no anesthesia, no problem. Cash only, please.

Thus it was that liquid silicone was pumped by the gallon into women's breasts by a variety of questionable physicians and nonphysicians. The only alternative that legitimate board-certified plastic surgeons had to offer was a fairly expensive surgical operation in which yet-to-be-popularized implants were placed in the breasts. This required an operation, an incision, some anesthesia, a recovery period, and a lot more expense. On balance, the injections looked more appealing.

A few years later, the problems began to show up, and they were serious ones. Silicone liquid, although fairly inert, rarely stayed where it was injected. It had the unwelcome habit of migrating around the body. Sometimes it just oozed into the soft tissues of the armpit or the upper abdomen, creating a swelling. Other times it traveled by means of the lymphatics into the bloodstream, where it circulated throughout the body. Liver, lungs, brain—it spread like metastatic cancer through similar pathways. On rare occasions, women died from strokes as the oily goo plugged up the circulation to the brain.

The most common problem, however, was the appearance of hard, deforming, painful lumps in the breasts. Some of them actually eroded through the skin, creating open, draining ulcerations. There was no way these could be distinguished from cancer by examination or mammography. Only a surgical biopsy of a lump could determine malignant from benign.

❖ *Silicone and the Showgirl*

Yvette was a glamorous French chorine performing in a gala revue in Las Vegas. She was the very embodiment of what a showgirl should have been: tall, leggy, beautiful, and kind, although the last quality was not a requirement for the job. One trait that was then (and is still) a requirement is the presence of a perfect bosom. Not too large, of course. These are not your North Beach topless dancers. Although frequently topless, showgirls must present themselves with a dancer's grace while carrying a twenty-pound headdress—jiggling not necessary.

All this was fine, except Yvette's figure was not endowed in that manner by nature. That was not a problem in Las Vegas in the late '60s; a trip to the local Silicone Man and *voilà!* a nice B cup in fifteen minutes before rehearsal. *Better living through chemistry.* She became the line captain, the lead chorus girl, and the star of the revue. She also met the man of her dreams, fell in love, and got married.

Several years later, she noticed a small ulceration in the skin near the left armpit. She was able to cover it with tape for the performance, but she was worried about it and sought out the man who had injected her. He was gone, disappeared. Address unknown.

She then consulted with a plastic surgeon in the city who advised her of the difficulties of silicone mastitis and treated her with antibiotics and DMSO, an interesting if simple chemical that had remarkable penetration through intact skin and very strong anti-inflammatory qualities. It was widely used in veterinary medicine but was relatively new and untried in humans. She got better. Not completely, but over the next few months the ulceration got smaller and smaller, and the firmness and redness reduced substantially.

And then it got worse.

When she came to see me, she had a hole almost two inches in diameter on the upper outer portion of the breast, near the armpit. She could no longer cover it for her work, and she had lost her job. The wound simply would not heal.

When I took her complete history, I was amazed to find that she had not had a biopsy performed of the area. She had been treated—and treated rather aggressively—for a presumed diagnosis of silicone mastitis, but no tissue sample had been examined under the microscope. This would be my first step. Unfortunately, it was also to be my last.

Breast cancer has several different tissue types, with critically differing prognoses. Medullary breast carcinoma, characterized by a florid inflammatory response to an invasive tumor, has a particularly poor one. It was my sad obligation to report this grave diagnosis to the patient and her husband. At first, they were dumbfounded, then furious at the time that had been wasted, and finally, mute in acceptance.

Yvette went through surgery, chemotherapy, and radiation therapy, only to die of metastatic disease within a year. Did the silicone injections cause her fatal cancer? Probably not. What they did cause was a complete obscuring of the presence of a cancer in the early stages, which, had it been treated one year earlier, might have resulted in her life being saved.

❖ *The Good News: Breast Implants*

Things have changed for the better. Today, augmentation of the female breast is performed routinely by means of a breast implant—a silicone bag filled with either saline (salt water) or a gel made of silicone polymer. The implants have their pros and cons, but they produce the desired result in a high percentage of cases. Plastic surgeons have had great success with this procedure in all its varied forms, and as a result, breast augmentation is currently the most popular operation in the country.

I believe that there may be yet a few famous movie stars in the sexy leading lady category who have *not* had breast implants. Of course, in the netherworld of "alternative" performers—exotic dancers, strippers, porn stars—breast augmentation is endemic, essential, and usually enormous. Even though women with small breasts can be extremely beautiful and sexy, there is almost no call for a small-breasted adult film star in the industry. Not surprisingly, aspiring male porn stars with small penises face a real challenge, and despite some ill-fated attempts, there's not a lot that plastic surgery can do for them.

Breast implants come in a huge variety of sizes and shapes. They are not sold as "B" or "C" cup size, but instead they're manufactured in sizes that correspond to their volume in milliliters. A very broad rule of thumb is that a 200 to 300 ml implant will add one cup size to the average breast.

Size matters, of course, and varies widely with the terrain. The average size implant in my practice is about 250 to 350 ml. A mere twenty miles away in Valencia, a colleague of mine puts in implants that *average* over 600 ml, which are twice the size of mine. And in the Midwest and the East Coast, 200 to 250 ml has been more common, but the influence of the West Coast is beginning to prevail even there.

The sizes speak for the diversity of desires among different subsets of women. Midwestern and East Coast women prefer not to have an obvious change, but West Coasters seem to prefer to be noticed. Many of the patients in my colleague's practice in Valencia work in the adult film industry centered in the nearby West San Fernando Valley, and they get paid to be noticed.

A well-known actress I had always admired came to see me for breast enlargement. Twenty years earlier, she had set the standard for the lean and leggy, long-haired brunette hippie dream. Despite the fact that she was nearly flat-chested at a time when voluptuousness held sway, she was an enormously popular sex symbol. Needless to say, I was surprised by her request.

"*You* want larger breasts?" I asked, trying not to look incredulous. "It will change your whole image." I pointed out that she had created a look that most women (and most men) would die for.

"Screw my image," she replied. "The thing is … no one ever asked me what I wanted for myself. And I want larger breasts, not huge, just big enough to make me feel a little more womanly."

I didn't say that I couldn't imagine anyone more womanly, but I thought it.

Regarding self-image, I've found personally and professionally that how you view yourself differs greatly from how the outside world views you. You can be full of insecurities about your appearance, while others think you are stunningly beautiful. This is particularly true in the entertainment world.

I did the operation as she requested, and she was very happy with the results. Curiously, whether she was simply shy about her new breasts or she consciously wanted to avoid changing her public image, she never wore anything very revealing. Her satisfaction came from knowing, not showing.

Breast implants today come in two basic types. Both consist of a soft silicone plastic shell; however, one is filled during surgery with saline (sterile salt water), and the other is prefilled with silicone gel. There are other variations, such as textured or smooth surface, high or low projection, round or teardrop shaped. The vast majority of implants are round in the front view and oval in the side view, and the most popular of them today are silicone gel–filled.

Silicone-filled implants intrinsically have a more natural feel to them than saline-filled ones. The gel flows more like the breast tissue that it is designed to enhance.

Because of some sensationalist bad press and a well-orchestrated effort on the part of the trial attorneys of America, silicone gel implants were banned in the United States by the FDA in the early '90s. Many millions of dollars in malpractice judgments and a $4.5 billion settlement to a global class action case have been cleverly wheedled out of unknowing juries by smart malpractice lawyers.

And now after many excellent scientific studies have been finished, after several million women have had the daylights scared out of them, after Dow-Corning has been forced into bankruptcy, the legal dust has finally settled, and it has become clear that whatever problems silicone implants may have, they don't appear to have any relationship to the life-threatening illnesses for which they had been blamed. Therefore, the use of silicone gel breast implants is again permitted, with more stringent reporting requirements and informed consents required.

An interesting observation about breast implants: here more than anywhere else, life imitates art. The large, artificially enhanced breasts seen in magazines, on TV, and in movies are now seen as the desired norm, and these images set the bar very high (and big) for the nonaltered woman. That which has been humanly created is viewed in some ways as the norm.

A wonderful exchange from the Steve Martin movie *LA Stories* comes to mind at this point. He is getting into bed with a young woman (Sarah Jessica Parker), and in the middle of his amorous excitement, he stops and sits up.

"I've never seen breasts like yours! They're so strange!" he remarks.

"That's because they're natural," she responds cheerfully.

A patient will commonly tell me that her worst fear about the procedure is that she will be too large, too obvious, too suggestive. She will inevitably say that she wants to be a C cup. Of course, a C cup in a five-foot, hundred-pound woman is very different than a C cup in a five-foot-eleven woman, so the actual implant size can be very different, too.

The fear of being too large is most common *before* the surgery. Afterward, when the preoperative anxiety, self-consciousness, and guilt (yes, guilt) have passed, many of my patients tell me wistfully that they might have liked to be a little bigger. On a few occasions, I've taken them back to the operating room several weeks later and put in larger implants. But so far, I have never had a patient unhappy because she ended up *too big*.

Discussions about size, type of implant, type of incision, and everything about the operation should be open and direct. If you are thinking of having breast implants, you should be able to tell your surgeon everything he or she needs in order to give you what you really want. It is an extremely personal decision, one in which your usual shyness or embarrassment should be left at the door. Particularly in matters of size, you might not get your wish unless you can talk openly.

Your reasons for wanting breast enhancement are personal, and they have everything to do with how your image impacts on yourself and others. Breast implants, like many plastic surgical operations, can be tremendously reinforcing and truly empowering to one's self-image and confidence.

A young rising-star actress had just completed her first major motion picture and felt in her bones that this was her breakthrough role. She correctly anticipated the gala openings and award shows to which she would be required to wear long elegant dresses with revealing décolletage as she walked up the red carpet. She moved with an easy, regal grace and looked incredible in anything from jeans to couture. But she told me she had a problem. Her breasts were rather petite, so she had worn padded, industrial-strength push-up bras throughout the filming. She imagined the comments: "Funny, she looked so sexy in the movie," or more to the point, "What happened to those boobs?" She needed to make her reality match the cinematic fantasy—a seemingly pragmatic rationale.

I couldn't shake the feeling that there might be more to it than this. Often, patients desiring plastic surgery feel guilty or scared, and rather than confront these feelings, they rationalize. Experience has taught me that it's important for a patient to be aware of and feel comfortable with their reasons for wanting surgery—whatever they may be—before the operation.

We spent a good deal of time talking, and finally, she acknowledged that she had always admired those more amply endowed actresses of the '50s and '60s and felt that this was a good opportunity to make her move in that direction. Her realization empowered her by transforming her decision from a worried reaction into a positive step she had always wanted to take. And so she had her breast augmentation, and she did indeed look wonderful walking down that red carpet ... and many red carpets since.

Regardless of how much attention you may draw to yourself from others, it's your own sense of self-fulfillment that is the richest beneficiary in the end. One of the most surprising and rewarding examples of this came early in my career and left me with a lasting impression.

❖ *Not Your Usual Breast Augmentation*

I'd been in practice in Beverly Hills for a few years when a woman came to see me for consultation about breast augmentation. This was becoming increasingly popular in the late '70s, although the implants were still in the early stages of development. Her request did not seem unusual. What was unusual and quite memorable about this patient was that she had severe kyphoscoliosis, a marked deformity of the torso. One shoulder was about eight inches higher than the other. There was an S-shaped curve to the thoracic and lumbar spine, and her legs were of such different proportions that she required a six-inch lift in one shoe just so she could walk.

To put it in popular usage, she was a hunchback. She was also a noted tenured professor of classic literature and humanities.

There is a certain comfort zone that most physicians slip into vis-à-vis the doctor-patient relationship. The patient comes seeking help, the doctor determines how best to give it. That easy relationship did not work with this patient, a woman of staggering intelligence and overwhelming physical deformity, requesting a purely cosmetic, seemingly frivolous procedure. Think of Stephen Hawking wanting a face-lift. It's doable, but...

I was at a loss. She sensed my hesitation.

"I know what you're thinking," she said.

I smiled nervously.

"Why would someone who looks like me want larger breasts?"

I said nothing, but she had me nailed. I felt strangely guilty.

"I just want them ... can't really explain it, but I know I'll feel better about myself. If it's not possible, that's okay, too."

As plastic surgeons, we are taught that a patient who has a great deal of concern about a tiny perceived defect is *not* a good surgical candidate. Here was a patient living every day with a deformity more crippling than most of us could ever imagine, who thought that implants would maybe make her feel better about herself. In short, she was an ideal patient from a psychological point of view.

But what about from a surgical point of view? Her distorted anatomy presented many real challenges. Would larger breasts merely emphasize her deformity? Should I position the implants so they would be level when she stands up? Or should I position them in proportion to her existing breasts, knowing that one would be much higher than the other?

I have learned over the years that when God created humans, He must have had many priorities that came before symmetry. Breast, eyes, ears—structures created in pairs are rarely symmetrical. The important thing is that the appearance *as a whole* is pleasing to behold.

My professor was anything but symmetrical, and nothing I could do would change that; however, I couldn't come up with a defensible reason **not** to operate. So I did. I inserted implants of slightly different sizes and slightly different positions to partially correct for symmetry, and she was extraordinarily happy.

The last time I saw her, there was a decided bounce in her difficult step, and I think she actually walked a little taller.

❖ Problems

Despite the fact that breast augmentation is a procedure with a fairly high rate of reoperation, most patients who have been interviewed say they are extremely pleased with the outcome and would do it again (and many do; as often as four or five times or more in their lifetime).

The most common complication after any operation is postoperative bleeding, occurring in less than 1 percent of the cases. This is not life-threatening bleeding (usually), but it is bleeding inside the wound (a *hematoma*). The breast may become very swollen, painful, and bruised. This requires a trip back to the operating room to reopen the wound under anesthesia, remove the clotted blood, cauterize or ligate any bleeding blood vessels, and then reclose the wound. This usually happens within the first twelve hours after surgery (a good justification for the aftercare facility), although I have seen it occur as late as one week afterward. *Properly treated, a hematoma has no negative long-term results.* There may be a longer, more intense period of bruising on the affected breast, but all will be well. Untreated, however, there will be prolonged healing time, considerably more pain, higher risk of infection, and an almost certain contracture of the scar capsule around the implant (see below) producing a hard, distorted breast.

The risk of hematoma is a very good reason to make sure your surgeon is equipped to handle any such contingencies. Ask yourself: Has he handled emergencies before? Does he take night calls? Does he charge an additional fee for such complications? Will he be able to use the same outpatient surgicenter that the original operation was performed in, or will it be necessary to go to the hospital with rather significant costs?

A young American woman living in Rome had a breast augmentation at the urging of her Italian boyfriend, who was an actor. Had I been her surgeon at the time, I would have counseled her to really think through her decision, for augmentation solely to make a man happy often has unhappy results.

While the operation was a success, it wasn't long before the boyfriend wanted them even bigger—an even bigger reason to reconsider the relationship. Obediently, she went back and had larger implants put in. One week later, her left breast swelled to triple the size of the right breast and became bruised and tender. She knew immediately that she had developed a hematoma. That's when she called me. She has also just discovered she was pregnant, and much to her sad surprise, her Romeo suggested she take a hike. He wanted nothing more to do with her. It was time to come home.

She flew to Los Angeles the next day. I had a car waiting at the airport to whisk her to my office. When she arrived, I took her straight into the operating room and removed the sizeable hematoma, leaving the implant in place. She did very well, and the results were good.

Afterward came the discussion about the wisdom of carrying a baby to term under the circumstances. Given that she had undergone two operations with anesthesia and drugs during the first trimester of uterine development, the likelihood of congenital deformities in the baby was significant. While many would have opted for an abortion as the prudent thing, she decided to have the baby. This story has a happy ending, for six months later, she gave birth to a perfectly normal baby.

Another possible complication of breast augmentation is permanent *numbness* in one or both nipples. There is a nerve—and sometimes several nerves—that comes from the spinal cord and gives sensation to the nipple. Their pathway is frequently unpredictable, and though we try very hard to avoid injuring them, permanent numbness may occur in about 1–2 percent of breasts. The frequency of numbness does not seem to be related to which incision site is used.

The most common reason for reoperation is the occurrence of *capsular contracture*, the tightening of the scar tissue casing around the implant, which can cause it to rise upward, become hard, misshapen, and sometimes painful. The simple presence of a scar capsule is not the problem, and in fact, that occurs in *all* patients. It is a normal physiologic response that our bodies try to "wall off" a foreign body, similar to the way an oyster will "wall off" a grain of sand and produce a pearl. Unlike the pearl, the breast implant scar capsule will be soft, filmy, and gossamer-thin, unless it begins to thicken and contract, most likely in response to a *low-grade infection* of the tissue around the implant. (See *"A Genuine Beverly Hills Princess."*)

This can happen at any time after the operation, and I have seen it occur days, weeks, months, or even years later. To help prevent capsular contracture, patients are instructed postoperatively to take antibiotics in situations when bacteria may enter the bloodstream, such as dental procedures or infections elsewhere in the body. Daily massage of the breasts is also recommended to stretch the capsule and keep it soft much like daily exercise strengthens and stretches muscles.

A great deal of work has gone into prevention of unacceptable contractures. In general, an implant placed deep to the pectoralis major muscle has a better chance of remaining soft than an implant placed above the muscle. This may be because of the constant massaging action of the muscle on the implant capsule or because the implant is more removed from the possibility of bacterial contamination. Many therapies are being investigated, but capsular contracture remains a vexing problem for some patients.

A portion of the work I do on a regular basis involves the removal and replacement of breast implants because of capsular contracture. Many women spend years with this condition, self-conscious about wearing anything too revealing, afraid to hug someone for fear their breasts will feel like two tennis balls. Some don't even acknowledge the condition to themselves.

Recently, a woman consulted with me about a face-lift. In the process of taking her history, I found that she had had breast augmentation twenty years earlier (not an uncommon incidental finding). I inquired if all was well with the implants. She responded wearily, saying that they were "as hard as rocks," but she was used to them. I asked if she ever considered having them replaced, and her response was that she was too fearful of the pain. "Besides," she said, "what good could be done? Aren't they always this hard?"

My patient was more than willing to have a face-lift, but she had given up completely on her hard breasts without ever having had a consultation. When I suggested that the implant technology and the operative style had changed rather dramatically over the last twenty years, she began to sound very interested and frankly excited.

I did perform a face-lift on her, and I also removed and replaced her old implants with their eggshell-like calcified capsules. It was clear that she was as delighted with her "new" soft breasts as she was with her more youthful countenance.

Oddly enough, even though removing and replacing an implant is more work than inserting it the first time around, there is usually much less pain, and the recovery is generally quicker. And although there are no guarantees that hardening will not recur, the operation removes the causes of the contracture and often produces a soft, natural, long-term result.

Aesthetic breast augmentation is here to stay, but it isn't for everyone. Maybe after you read this chapter and weigh the pros and cons, you'll decide that the Wonderbra is more to your liking. Maybe you burned your bra in the '60s and couldn't care less. But if you are interested, don't be shy. Don't be ashamed. Above all, don't be impulsive. Look into it with a qualified surgeon. Ask the questions, get the answers (you've read some of mine), and take your time. Recognize that you might have ambivalent feelings, a common experience in anyone seeking aesthetic surgery. And if it adds up on balance, go for it. It's not by chance that it's become the most popular plastic surgery procedure of the year.

The truth is that you never know how the people in your life will respond to your having breast augmentation. Often, there is a very pleasant surprise. To that end, let me leave you with this anecdote:

I had a patient who was the only female partner in a prestigious law firm, specializing in prosecuting sexual harassment cases. She was a stalwart of the feminist movement, and she was very stressed by her secret, unrelenting desire to have breast augmentation.

"My colleagues will ridicule me!" she sighed. I refrained from offering too much encouragement, knowing that she would be in a tight spot if she indeed lost credibility with her friends and colleagues.

After weeks of intense internal debate, she went ahead with the surgery. Her augmentation was a great success. Ironically, the decision to tell anyone about her surgery was harder than her decision to actually have the surgery. After she finally worked up the courage, she very hesitantly revealed her secret to her innermost circle of friends. As it turned out, they shocked her even more than she shocked them. Their unanimous, enthusiastic response? "You go, girl!"

CHAPTER FIVE
I KNEW THERE'D BE DAYS LIKE THIS

❖ *Celebrities Behaving Badly*

We've all seen famous celebrities in bad situations. In fact, some of the highest-rated TV shows thrive on such news. It seems to be a prerequisite to adulthood that famous young hipsters go through a series of problems involving drugs, alcohol, DUI arrests, sexual misbehaving, or all of the above. They usually have enough money and influence to get away with infractions that would put most of us in jail. Rarely will anyone in their retinue tell them that they ought to behave themselves, lest they be ejected from the inner circle. Besides, the weekly magazines wouldn't exist without the usual posed shots of these slim young beauties walking down red carpets or the candid shots of one sitting in his or her wrecked Mercedes, looking stunned and stoned.

After surviving some of the above travails, many artists begin to search for a greater meaning to life. They become spokespersons for a variety of causes, lending their fame to hot-button candidates or worthy causes in the increasingly polarized liberal-conservative conflicts: AIDS, abortion rights, gay rights, right to life, Iraq, Darfur, legalizing marijuana, etc. And many react to their previously dissolute lives by becoming hardcore teetotalers, exercise addicts, and health food and supplement junkies. Some vigorously proselytize their newfound lifestyle to the rest of us junk-food-eating, exercise-loathing couch potatoes. Drug addiction becomes tofu addiction. Cynicism and hypocrisy inevitably raise their ugly heads.

It's all too easy to sneer at hypocrisy. To an extent, it's a normal human frailty. We all want to have great schools and health care, but we don't want to pay the increased taxes required to fund them. We want to conserve energy and protect the environment, but really, do we want to swelter without air-conditioning on a hot muggy day? We want to grow old gracefully, but *what about these lines on my face, Doctor?*

Most of us manage to deal with the hypocrisy in our daily lives, but when the hypocrisy is being dished out by a seriously high-minded celebrity who's mostly famous for simply being famous, my Midwestern funny bone is tickled.

The setup:

Several years ago, one of my young starlet patients, a very confirmed and openly proselytizing vegan, was in my waiting room, hunched over a small bottle of a skin care product we sell in our clinic, reading the fine print. She furrowed her pretty brow in disapproval, shook her head, and announced to all in my waiting room, "I wouldn't even consider using this product. It contains parabens, and everyone knows they're poisonous."

The truth is that parabens have been around as preservatives in cosmetics and skin care products for generations, and they are found naturally in blueberries, among other foods. There have been some questions raised in the alternative medical literature about potential harmful side effects, but these have been discredited by well-controlled scientific studies from academics around the world. Please note: this is not a vast right-wing conspiracy cooked up by drug firms. I don't believe any developed nation in the world seriously has considered limiting the use of parabens. But for my patient, it was the gospel: *anything containing parabens must be clearly and decisively shunned.* She stood erect, turned on her red-soled pumps with a silent *harrumph!* and stormed out.

The punch line:

Barely outside the glass door, she stopped, took a cigarette from her handbag, and lit up, taking a long and satisfying drag. She walked off briskly, leaving a trail of blue-white smoke behind her, with the front office staff and patients shaking their heads in puzzled amusement.

Listen up, people! Today's lesson would be the following: Parabens ... bad. Nicotine and tar ... good. Go figure.

Even the cigarette industry was forced to acknowledge the addictive properties and carcinogenicity of those by-products of smoking. I'm certain that if I had asked her about her seemingly conflicting choices, she would have told me that it was okay, she was smoking an *organic* cigarette, which I'm guessing only has organic nicotine and tar.

Now for a confession about my own hypocrisy: there are no parabens in my own Leaf & Rusher line of skin care products. Why? It's not simply because there are other equally effective preservatives; it's mostly because those equally effective preservatives don't carry the paraben *stigma*. Marketing experts teach us, "Perception is everything."

As I said, a little hypocrisy is part of the human condition. I'm not immune.

❖ *Selling Plastic Surgery*

The commercial, business aspects of my specialty were not at all of concern when I began to practice. I loved the work and found that I was good at it, and my satisfied patients referred friends. That was the traditional, widely accepted way for doctors and other professional people to develop a successful practice.

Not anymore. It's all changed. Everything is about marketing, particularly in the case of newer plastic surgeons trying to establish a practice. The competition becomes fiercer with each new crop of graduating residents, and the means by which they "get their names out there" are somewhat lacking in taste or professionalism, to put it kindly.

There are billboards along the San Diego Freeway that advertise "Breast Implants $2999!" Cable TV ads display smiling, effusive postoperative patients and doctors explaining how easy it is to achieve the face-lift of one's dreams. Glossy ads, usually in the back pages of regionally-distributed magazines, exclaim the merits of a unique-sounding "trademarked" operation that only this particular doctor has the skills to perform. Mercedes and Bentleys with vanity license plates like FACE UP, or LIFTING, or BOOBS 4U cruise along the boulevards. Health care reform is already here.

Our national plastic surgery meetings have both scientific sessions and commercial exhibitors. In the past, these exhibitors were mainly offering new surgical instruments, sutures, injectable fillers, and the like. Now about 50 percent of them are all about marketing techniques, mostly centering on the Internet. The reason for the big push in marketing is to help the growing numbers of plastic surgeons (and would-be "cosmetic surgeons") gain an edge in their competition for patients.

I've been lucky. Because I've been in practice for quite a few years, I've managed to mostly sidestep this carnival of PR and advertising. That doesn't mean I totally ignore the growing competition with my otherwise collegial associates. I just prefer to compete on a more professional level, in ways that don't appear too commercial or self-serving.

But I compete.

When Jay Leno's *Tonight Show* was at its apex, I got a call from the producer in the weeks before Christmas. She told me that Jay was going to do a "Winter Wonderland" show for the holidays. Truckloads of snow were to be brought in from the nearby mountains and dumped in the NBC parking lot in Burbank—Jay wanted the viewers to see that even in sunny Southern California we can have the enjoyment of winter sports.

She asked me if I would be interested in performing a nose job on a snowman.

The pause on my end of the line must have urged her to continue.

"We will have a big snowman with a big carrot for a nose, and we thought it would be funny if a real plastic surgeon, like you, Dr. Leaf, would take a big lopping shears and chop off the end of it on the show."

Another pause. I thought that this sounded a little ... unprofessional. *Sure it would be funny, and Jay would be able to create something really hilarious with it. But ...*

"It's okay if you don't want to do it, Dr. Leaf; we understand it's not necessarily your thing."

Then she added, " We can get Dr. Glassman to do it." Harry Glassman was a colleague of mine, an accomplished plastic surgeon, and a friend.

"What time would you like me to show up? Should I wear my white coat?"

"Yes, please. Also we're going to have you pretend to do liposuction on the snowman. Can you bring a liposuction cannula with you?"

"No problem." So much for professonalism.

I did the show, and it was great fun. No one has ever consulted me for a snowperson rhinoplasty as a result of that broadcast, but I really do know how to do one.

I compete.

❖   The Long and the Short of It

Cliff was an audio engineer at a prominent recording studio, a techno-nerd, a tall, awkward man in his midthirties with an unruly mop of unkempt, oily black hair, wire-rimmed glasses perched on a long, thin nose, and a plaid flannel shirt with pocket protector. He wasn't the typical Beverly Hills plastic surgery patient. And although looks can be deceiving, his were not. What he wanted from me dealt more with function than form, and it would never be seen in public. Probably.

When Cliff was twenty-three years of age, he had undergone circumcision. Adult circumcision was not very common in the United States of the late twentieth century, and his had gone badly. The doctor who had performed the procedure was not experienced, and as a result, Cliff's foreskin had been cut at a very noticeable angle. The top of the foreskin was short and looked like any other circumcised penis, but the portion of the foreskin on the undersurface of the penis looked as if it had been missed totally by the surgeon's instruments. In fact, it projected beyond the head of the penis. Cliff's complaints were not about the appearance, but more, as Cliff put it, because it made intercourse and masturbation difficult. And although the appearance was not his chief complaint, it was not very far below it.

The kicker in Cliff's history was that he had already seen approximately thirty doctors, plastic surgeons, urologists, and general surgeons. All of them had reportedly told him that nothing could be done to help him.

One of the first rules of plastic surgery is that if a patient tells you thirty experts who make their living doing surgery had declined to repair something that appeared simple, you ought to think twice about accepting the job. But I was young, idealistic, and determined to avoid clichés about Beverly Hills plastic surgeons. Here was a man suffering from a correctable disease (in a sense) and I, the healer of the sick, was going to heal him. And I did ... eventually.

It looked embarrassingly easy—just a little trim of the excess foreskin to match the normal portion. After all, pediatricians, obstetricians, and even rabbis did this on a daily basis—to newborns. The problem with adults was that tension on the skin of the penis was immensely higher during erection. If I trimmed the skin so it would be nice and even while the penis was flaccid, as it always is when anesthetized, the sutures might break and cause a considerable wound healing problem if an erection occurred during the healing phase. And worse, if too much skin was resected, a permanent and painful deformity could occur during future episodes of arousal.

Thinking creatively, I decided to enlist Cliff's aid in determining the correct amount to remove. I gave him a surgical skin marking pen and suggested he go home, get an erection in the privacy of his own surroundings (not an insurmountable challenge for him), and then mark the amount of excess foreskin. If he felt it wasn't sure of the amount of skin to be removed, he didn't need to worry. The marking pen could be erased by wiping the lines with an alcohol pad, and I gave him a supply of those to take. He left my office with a happy optimism. He had his marker, his wipes, and an appointment for surgery with his new doctor, and he was empowered.

He returned on the scheduled morning, and I immediately knew when he walked in that something was terribly wrong. He was pacing in the waiting room, sweating heavily, and wringing his hands. It's not uncommon for patients to be nervous on the day of surgery, but this reaction was way past nervous and well into panic.

I brought him into my office and asked him what was wrong. He responded by standing up, lowering his trousers, and pointing at his penis. There, where the normal glans (head) should be, was something that looked like a Roma tomato—red, swollen beyond recognition, and intensely inflamed. Apparently in the throes of insecurity, Cliff had marked, erased, marked again, and erased again, *ad infinitum*. He had rubbed his penis with enough alcohol to take the paint off his car. I felt horrible and embarrassed for him, and I realized that asking patients to shoulder responsibility for their surgical planning was probably not a great idea. I cancelled the surgery, gave him some topical anti-inflammatory cream, some prednisone pills to quickly remove the inflammation, and a heartfelt apology.

Happily, after a few weeks when the inflammation had gone, I took Cliff and his penis into the OR and did a conservative partial recircumcision, and all turned out well. I don't know if he wound up living happily ever after, but if he didn't, he can't blame it on his foreskin.

❖ *Alternative Plastic Surgery*

A plate of brown rice and some tofu, herbal estrogen replacement therapy, acupuncture, acupressure, reflexology, antiaging clinics, human growth hormone, biofeedback, and high colonics— "Alternative Medicine" has become not so alternative and much more mainstream. This is particularly true in Southern California and New York, where the latest New Thing is accepted as gospel until it is totally trashed by the Next Latest New Thing. Most of these once-suspect treatments now enjoy a reasonable level of credibility, and even Big Insurance is reluctantly starting coverage for them, the ultimate sign of acceptance.

The medical usage of marijuana still evokes a huge amount of skepticism. I personally think that legalizing pot for medical *and* nonmedical usage would eliminate most of the drug crimes in the country, saving taxpayers millions of dollars and bringing billions of legal dollars into the state and federal coffers through taxation, not unlike regular cigarettes and liquor. About twenty-five years ago, I wasn't quite so certain of this libertarian-sounding position. That's when I met Morrie.

He was a New York talent agent. That title says almost everything. He was an AA-type personality, smoking and drinking his way through the 24/7 high-power world of the recorded music industry. He lived way to the left of the fast lane in Manhattan, and he knew every person with a tattoo or facial piercing east of the Hudson. His day began around 6:00 PM and ended sometime after the last drink and the last set of the last band in the last club in town. Then one day, Morrie, fresh from a coronary bypass and a divorce, and sick and tired of the stressful life in the city, decided to hang it up and move out to sunny, laid-back Los Angeles.

Los Angeles, a city divided by racial, societal, and financial boundaries, is also divided by a mountain range. The Santa Monica Mountains are not much in terms of height, but what they lack in altitude, they make up for in traffic congestion.

Even in the early '80s, many people lived in the San Fernando Valley and worked in the city. The freeways were usually tied up at rush hour, and besides, they were usually out of the way. The most direct route to the Valley was then (and is now) the canyons. So these beautiful, residential, tree-lined winding roads were bumper-to-bumper twice a day in both directions, but it was still better than trudging over to the congested freeways.

The hillsides were forested with pine and eucalyptus trees. Stilt-supported cantilevered houses could be seen peeking through the treetops. You could almost believe you were in Colorado except for the traffic. The different canyons also had their own personalities: Benedict Canyon and Coldwater Canyon led to Beverly Hills and were a little snooty; Beverly Glen was more hippie, and Laurel Canyon was more artsy.

Morrie drove across the country in his Mercury Marquis all by himself, a leisurely weeklong journey. He arrived in February of 1982 and rented a house in Laurel Canyon. The day after he moved in, the rains began.

People say that there are no seasons in Los Angeles, but that's not true. We have the fire season, the rainy season, the mudslide season, the earthquake season, and summer, the smog season. After the Santa Ana winds from the desert have dessicated the hillside brush and shrubs, the resultant tinder is an easy target for an accidental spark, a lightning bolt, or an arsonist's match. The inevitable brush fires leave the clay soil with nothing to hold it together, and the rains that follow create major mudslides. That particular year, the rains and mudslides were more intense than usual, and LA neophyte Morrie was no match for them.

He was driving his Mercury through a torrential downpour heading up Laurel Canyon. He had been shopping for supplies to furnish his newly rented home, which he had moved into the previous day. The car was loaded with still-packed luggage and household supplies when it began to lose some traction on the water-soaked pavement. Another point about LA roads: with no rain for ten to eleven months, all the road oil and grease soaks into the pavement, waiting for the rains to bring it to the surface. Morrie's Mercury began to slide backward down the hill. It gained speed as it approached the steepest part of the grade, and then, completely out of control, flew off the curve into a deep gulley. Morrie was thrown out of the car, sustaining several broken ribs, a concussion, and abrasions and lacerations of his face, arms, and legs.

He was carried out of the canyon by ambulance workers and brought to Cedars Sinai Hospital. While his wounds were being cleaned and dressed, he suffered a cardiac arrest. He was successfully resuscitated and admitted to the ICU, where it became evident that his kidneys had stopped functioning. An arteriovenous shunt was placed in his arm to enable him to undergo renal dialysis, which could buy time for his kidneys to recover function. And eventually, after three weeks in ICU, his physicians called me to help with his wound care.

Morrie's wounds were not life-threatening. His condition had stabilized, but he had large patches of partial- to full-thickness skin loss on his legs and buttocks. The wounds had not been the priority in the previous few weeks, and the time had come to repair them. He was still too fragile to take to the operating room, put under general anesthesia, remove the dead tissue, and place skin grafts. Instead, his care became that of daily visits, bedside debridement (trimming away of dead tissue), and repeated dressing changes over match-head-sized "pinch" skin grafts, performed under local anesthesia .

Morrie and I got to know each other well over the next month, and his progress was painful and slow. He had lost a great deal of weight from his already thin frame, and he looked more fragile and depressed by the day.

I took a four-day weekend vacation around six weeks after I had begun Morrie's care. The day I returned, I went to Cedars to check on Morrie. I walked up to the door of his room, knocked, and started to walk in.

I stopped. There was a healthy-looking younger man in what had been Morrie's room. I quickly apologized for barging into the wrong room and went to the nursing station to inquire after Morrie's whereabouts. I was worried, because he had looked extremely frail when I had last seen him, and I feared the worst.

The nurse gave me an odd look and reassured me that Morrie had not been moved. I returned to the room and reentered tentatively. At the same instant that I knew it was indeed him, I noted a peculiar but recognizable scent in the room. He looked up at me, smiling.

"Hi, Doc."

"Morrie, what's that you've got behind your back?"

I knew Morrie was hiding a joint—a futile gesture, especially with the bluish cloud of smoke curling around his smiling face. He started laughing at my first puzzled and then disapproving smile.

"What're they gonna do, Doc? Arrest me? I've already been dead once!"

I looked at him more critically; he looked great. He had shaved, showered, and dressed himself in clean pajamas, and it appeared that blood was running through his body in a much more vigorous manner. His wounds were finally healing well. His kidneys had recovered, and his appetite was amazing. I would have loved to take some credit for his remarkable recovery, but I knew, as did everyone else on that floor, that he probably had received as much help from his dealer as he did from his doctors.

Morrie continued to improve rapidly, and he was discharged a week later. He came to my office for follow-up after another week, and he looked wonderful. He was dressed in a dark suit, a white shirt with a tie and gold cufflinks. He looked like the perfect picture of a successful businessman. I commented that he looked very New York today, as opposed to the more casual garb usually seen in Los Angeles.

"Funny you should mention that, Doc," he said. And then he told me he had decided to move back to New York, where the climate fit his clothes and temperament. He had had more than enough of laid-back LA. The hurly-burly concrete canyons and honking taxis of NYC were more calming to him than the mountains and valleys of the Golden State.

"Besides," he continued, "Manhattan is one place I'll never have to drive a car again."

❖ Mob Doc

One day two gentlemen from Colombia came to my office. One was wearing an expensive-looking dark blue suit, white shirt, and dark tie. He was the interpreter. The patient he accompanied wore a loose-fitting Hawaiian shirt over dark slacks, and both men sported an unusual (for daytime) amount of heavy gold jewelry.

I inquired politely about the reason for the visit, although I presumed it had to do with the oddly-shaped nose he was sporting, one of the most misshapen I'd ever seen. (The only one worse than this resulted from a patient dropping a 200-pound barbell on his nose while bench-pressing. He was extremely lucky to be alive.)

I've learned over the years that one must not presume why a patient is seeking consultation; it is very awkward to begin talking to a patient about their nose and be met with a blank stare, or worse, an embarrassed reply, "What's wrong with my nose? I wanted to see you about my eyes!" or something similar. In this case, there was no surprise in his request.

The history, given by the interpreter in guarded, measured responses to my questions, was that he had been struck on the side of his nose in an accident about a year ago. When I queried about the type of accident, the two men looked at each other, and there was an animated discussion in rapid Pidgin-Spanish. It seemed to me that the translator was trying to convince the patient to explain the circumstances of the injury, but the patient was having reservations about being specific. He did, however, manage to make it very clear that I was the anointed one who they had selected to do the surgery, because I had done a similar procedure on their friend about ten years previously. (I had no recollection of that incident.) Also, he didn't care what my fee might be, but he insisted on paying in cash.

While they were arguing how best to describe the accident, I couldn't help but notice the imposing strength and menacing nature of the two dark, simian-browed men before me, their hands thick and calloused. Even with their clothes, I could easily appreciate the huge necks and powerful arms and barrel chests. And was that an odd bulge under the interpreter's left arm? I began to feel uneasy.

Eventually, my patient was persuaded to report that his nose was injured with the butt of a gun during a fight—an AK47 assault rifle, to be precise. Once the secret was out, they wanted to let me know everything about the injury, including a mimed reenactment. I didn't really need to know much more detail than that. I figured that as long as they wanted me to help, I was safe.

I focused on the physical examination. The upper portion of the nose, the bony pyramid, was absent, having been totally smashed inward. In profile, the contour started normally between the eyebrows and then dipped suddenly inward where the nasal bones should have been, and finally, a sharp outward thrust at the tip. This is often referred to as a "saddle deformity" for obvious reasons. Aside from the grotesque appearance, there was nothing to support his reading glasses, and he could only breathe through his mouth. His nasal septum, the wall between the two nostrils, was almost totally absent. This part of the deformity might have been caused by the trauma, but it's most commonly the result of a long-standing, heavy-duty cocaine habit.

Several things immediately came to mind:

a. This was a complex injury, probably a result of both a blunt trauma and cocaine erosion.

b. I would need to put some structural material like bone, cartilage, or a synthetic silicone strut under the skin to support it.

c. There was no way to reconstruct the nasal septum—it was too far gone—but if I could provide support to the bridge of the nose, he should be able to breathe more freely, and it would certainly look much better.

d. This is a Colombian drug-dealing, cocaine-snorting, cash-carrying killer, and I would be crazy to operate on him.

e. If I didn't accept him as a patient, he or his friend might get angry.

f. If I did accept him and had a complication, I would be in *agua caliente.*

g. I was in a tight spot.

Drawing upon my background experiences as chief resident in surgery at the University of Chicago and the gangland clientele we frequently served, I was able to recall that the doctors were always considered "untouchable" by the gang members. I was hoping that such a courtesy extended naturally from the south side of Chicago to the jungles of Medellin. I took a deep breath and started explaining what the anatomical problem was and how I might be able to improve it. With all my patients, I am careful not to suggest perfection for fear of not meeting their expectations. With Senor Gonzales (not his real name—what am I, crazy?), I was even more cautions, for obvious reasons. He listened attentively to his translator and asked questions, and despite my concerns, I felt the establishment of the doctor-patient relationship forming.

It has always been a surprise to me that the most worldly, the most intelligent, the most powerful, and even the most menacing people all seem quite reasonable when they are sitting in the patient's chair. They become aware that no matter how many people worship or fear them, they are facing an operation whose success depends largely on their surgeon. It's time for one's best behavior. As the potential surgeon, I'm also aware of the frighteningly rapid transformation that may take place after the surgery is over. The patient that is the most solicitous and most flattering before surgery is likely to be the most angry and litigious afterward if he or she is not completely satisfied.

In Senor Gonzales's situation, it wasn't a lawsuit I was worried about. It's a precariously narrow path to tread.

A few weeks later, after I had obtained medical clearance from a trusted internist, after I had thought several times about an FBI inquiry and discarded the idea, I did the operation. The goal was to recreate the bridge of the nose and add support like a roof beam under a sagging roof. For this, one needs some firm tissue, and with such a traumatic deformity, it would be best to put in living tissue, probably a graft from the patient himself rather than a piece of silicone plastic, which would likely become infected and have to be removed. I chose the safer path in this case.

Most commonly, these grafts are cartilage, which is flexible and carveable, or bone. Both are usually tolerated very well for many years, perhaps permanently. The usual sources for obtaining cartilage are the nasal septum (his was gone), the ear (his looked like cauliflower), or the rib. In his case, the rib was chosen by default: the other sources were not available.

The procedure went smoothly, and the results were better than I had hoped for and better than he was prepared for, too. He paid me the ultimate compliment. He disappeared after the splint came off, and I never heard from him again. My fears about being forced into becoming the attending plastic surgeon to the cartel were overwrought.

Not a postcard, nothing. Amen.

❖   *Is the Doctor In ... or Out?*

One of the reasons people become doctors is to somehow ease their own fear of disease. The flip side of this fear is the infinite susceptibility to *imagined* illness. It's frightening to study a variety of diseases in medical school and to realize that you are experiencing some of the same symptoms—the so-called "medical student's disease." All of us have had this in one form or another, especially with illnesses that have the vaguest presenting symptoms. Lupus, TB, Guillan-Barre syndrome—these among others begin with undistinguished, poorly defined signs of tiredness, malaise, mild aches, and pains, and then can progress to serious, sometimes lethal outcomes.

The study of tropical diseases is, far and away, the scariest and the most morbidly fascinating of all. Yaws, schistosomiasis, leprosy, and the particularly macabre guinea worm are the stuff that bad dreams are made of. Their prevalence in Africa only adds to the bizarre nature of these syndromes, but they are so alien that it was hard to imagine that I myself was suffering from any of them. They were all *over there*, and I was *over here*. Thus, I was out of harm's way from those frightening sicknesses.

The granddaddy of all medical-student-imagined ailments is, of course, the brain tumor. Have you ever had a headache? Lightheadedness? Lethargy? Tingling in the extremities? Rushing sounds in the ears? Blurriness of vision? Then you've got it! Fortunately, these are also symptoms of the most common ailments that we are faced with every day, including stress and mild viral infections. Most of us graduate medical school and find that we have nothing to worry about except paying back our student loans.

I had a brief "brain tumor" experience once on my way to work, well past the time when I should have known better. I was driving to work—a distance of only about two miles—when I began to feel very sluggish and slow-witted. I also had a bit of a headache. Fortunately, I was not on one of southern California's famed freeways, but I was creeping slowly down Coldwater Canyon in light traffic. I noted, with a strange calmness, that I had just lightly bumped into the rear bumper of the car in front of me. Apparently, the driver didn't notice, or at least didn't say anything, so I shook my head and blinked a few times and continued my short drive into town and made my way into my parking lot. How could that have happened? Was I in some altered state? It suddenly became crystal clear; I had a brain tumor.

As I was walking up the stairs from the underground parking lot with heavy, measured steps, my concerns about the BT or perhaps merely meningiococcal meningitis were replaced by the dawning recognition that I must have accidentally taken a sleeping pill instead of my thyroid pill that morning. I had been taught that elderly people had a great deal of trouble with their medications, but I was just on the north side of forty and should have known better.

I arrived in the office, realizing that whatever surgery case was waiting for me would have to be cancelled. As bad luck would have it, my patient, the teenage son of a major movie actor, was already on the operating table, awaiting his rhinoplasty. He was not yet anesthetized, but he had an IV already running in his arm, sedation on board (like me), and a very anxious celebrity mother pacing in the waiting room. Fading fast, I explained to my nurses what had happened and arranged for them to discontinue the anesthesia and cancel the case. Then I went to explain to the mother.

I have always felt that honesty is the best policy. In retrospect, it would have been better to offer up my brain tumor diagnosis, but instead I explained as apologetically as I could while only slightly slurring my speech that I had inadvertently medicated myself as well as her son that morning. As I vaguely sensed a volcano about to erupt, I mumbled more words of apology, stumbled into my office, closed the door, and passed out on my sofa.

I awoke refreshed several hours later and immediately began to worry about the likelihood that I would be branded an addict or some other form of impaired character. What could I do to salvage my reputation? I tried repeatedly to call my patient's mother and explain, but I reached only the answering machine. Despite my most woeful apologies, she never called me back—at least not immediately,

About twelve years later, she called and made an appointment to see me. She appeared in my office at the appointed time, as if nothing had happened, to consult with me about a face-lift. I self-consciously avoided the subject of her son's almost-nose-job fiasco during the consultation.

After completing the examination, I summoned up my bravery and asked her about him. She remembered the incident clearly and started laughing, which I took as a very good sign. As it turned out, they had decided together that my mishap was a sign that he shouldn't have the surgery after all.

He had grown up just fine. In fact, she wanted a face-lift because she wanted to look good at his wedding. He was happy, healthy, and handsome, and I didn't have a brain tumor.

❖ *Twins*

Investigative plastic surgeons always dream of nature offering a perfectly controlled laboratory experiment: a pair of identical twins, one living in England and one living in sunny southern California. They live apart for twenty or thirty years, both taking good care of themselves, eating well, exercising regularly, not smoking, and at about fifty years of age, they come in together to see me for consultation. What differences would I expect to see?

As predictably as night follows day, the one living in England will have much smoother skin, fewer lines, less pigment changes than her LA sister. And given the one variable outlined, the only reason for the difference is the respective climates they each inhabited and, more specifically, the amount of sun exposure they received during the period in question. (The dream situation does not include the possibility that the English sister spent her summers in the South of France.)

A recent study in the journal *Plastic and Reconstructive Surgery* examined the twins phenomenon scientifically. There is a huge convention of identical twins every year in Twinsburg, Ohio. Thousands of pairs come together for a few days of fun. The plastic surgery team from Case Western Reserve University in Cleveland set up a booth there to study how different lifestyles affected identical twins. A specialized camera was used to take pictures of each twin under identical lighting, magnification, etc. Then the twins filled out a questionnaire describing their habits, with particular attention to smoking, sun exposure, drugs, stress levels, etc. The sets of photos were then judged by independent observers, rating how much older one twin looked than the other.

The findings were very impressive. They showed that smoking

adds about two to three years of perceived age, and that sun exposure was similar. Extra weight could go either way. Genetics can only influence appearance so far. The twin who lives a healthier life inevitably appears more youthful.

I had such an experience, with a slightly different twist. The twins were born in the South and grew up together until they were in their early twenties when one of them left, moved to Los Angeles, and became a television star, which required her to take good care of herself, avoid sun and smoking, and exercise regularly. The other twin stayed home, became a schoolteacher, smoked a bit, had two children, and really didn't pay much attention to any kind of sun protection. In short, she lived a pretty normal life.

Miss A, the TV star, came to see me in her late forties. She was beautiful and in great shape, but she felt the need for a face-lift and eyelid surgery in order to keep her edge on the series she was working in. I agreed and performed her face-lift and eyelid repair. She had a beautiful, extremely natural result.

A year later, she revealed to me that she was in fact an identical twin and wanted her sister to come out and have a face-lift as a birthday present. When Mrs. B arrived, I was stunned by the similarity of the two, but Mrs. B looked like Miss A's mother. Mrs. B was slightly overweight, had taken no pains to color her hair, and was not on comfortable speaking terms with makeup. She was a natural woman, a handsome woman, who in any other situation would be perfectly fine, but next to her twin, it was like day and night.

This was going to be fun. Mrs. B had her face-lift, and with the help of some of Miss A's friends in the beauty business, she had her hair colored and styled, her makeup done, her brows shaped, her diet corrected, and *voilà!* she became a supporting actress on the same show, working as Mrs. A's evil twin for the summer. In the fall, she returned home to continue teaching, with a new hazard to deal with.

The other teachers and parents and especially the students all wanted her autograph. Two months of fame can be irresistible.

Another interesting thing about twins is that if they both are subject to the same operation, they should respond the same. If one gets one type of medication for pain and swelling and the other gets a placebo, then any differences would be statistically significant. Or so I thought.

❖   *The Experiment*

Bart and Bert were identical twin brothers, both twenty-two years old, and they were gorgeous. They had thick black hair, glittering dark eyes and strong brows, curved lips and strong chins, and bodies out of *Men's Fitness*. The only perceived flaw—and it was not much of a flaw—was seen in their identically hooked noses. There was also an unperceived flaw; I had the gnawing suspicion that their combined IQs totaled less than one hundred. They had come to Los Angeles to seek their fame in the movie business, and they had been told that they needed to get rid of their ethnic-looking noses to make it in the big time. So they came to me, and I had an idea.

Identical twins are nature's experimental subjects. Two sets of identical genes offer a perfect setup to compare therapies, surgeries, and much more. At the time, I was examining the possible benefit of giving a patient nonsteroidal anti-inflammatory medication before an operation, to see if it reduced their postoperative pain. If one group of patients received Motrin or Ibuprofen preoperatively and the other group received a placebo, then it would simply be a matter of counting the pain pills used by the two separate groups after the surgery to determine the effectiveness.

A pair of twins provided the perfect matched controls. I would give Bart the real Motrin, and I would give Bert the placebo. Then they would both have the same rhinoplasty by the same surgeon (me), and we would count the pain pills they each used postoperatively to see what difference it had made. I explained the plan clearly, so they were aware they were participating in an experiment. They would not know if they were getting the real pill or the fake one. I was aware that one pair of subjects did not make a statistically significant study, but it should have clearly demonstrated a *trend*. (My statistics professor used to say there are three kinds of lies: white lies, black lies, and trends.)

Then we began, and I had every hope that this would produce some meaningful information. I thought I had considered every possible contingency. The only error I made was in assuming that I was dealing with two human beings of somewhat normal intelligence. They say that twins are different, and these two certainly were. To begin with, they put all their preoperative pills in one bottle so they could remind each other to take them according to the schedule. Then they did the same with their pain pills. In the end, none of us could tell which pills either had taken.

They both turned out fine, even more handsome than before. I have no idea if they ever made it in the movies. They were definitely more Tweedledum and Tweedledee than the Olson twins.

CHAPTER SIX
FACE-LIFTS

❖ *You Only See the Bad Ones*

"I never thought I'd consider a face-lift."

"I always thought I'd age gracefully."

"I look in the mirror, and suddenly, I see my mother."

"I don't want to look like all these bad face-lifts you see walking around in Beverly Hills."

That last comment isn't really fair. I see overdone, inappropriately tight faces everywhere—New York, Paris, Chicago, Milan—but Beverly Hills always gets a bum rap. That's at least partially because there are so many plastic surgeons, both real and bogus, in this concentrated little area. Some of these surgeons are keen, intuitive, and adept in their work, but others don't have a clue. The latter have no training and do the same inadequate operation on anyone careless enough to submit to their procedures.

In such a mixed milieu, one's perceptions are skewed. There is one axiom to remember, and only one: *Good plastic surgery is invisible. You only see the bad ones.*

Unfortunately, there are so many visible examples of bad face-lifts that observers may conclude that this is the way a face-lift is supposed to look. The truth is that bad face-lifts, like bad toupees, are apparent to everyone except (mercifully) the people who own them.

What makes a *good* face-lift? It might be easier to describe what makes a bad one.

Scars: You really shouldn't be able to see them without good light and close inspection. Even with that, the scars are pretty hard to find. The scar should hug the curve of the front of the ear and even go into the ear canal a little at the *tragus* (the little bump right in front of the ear canal). Some surgeons place the scar totally in front of the ear. You can get away with this once in a while, but it usually creates a scar that's a complete giveaway. Behind the ear, if needed, the scar should lie directly in the ear crease, going up quite high before curving backward into the hair. If the scar is placed *beneath* the hairline behind the ear, it then becomes visible and requires that the patient always wear her hair down to cover it.

There's more, too. Even if the scar is placed behind the tragus, the skin must be sutured with *no tension*. If the cheek is sutured under even a small amount of tension, it will pull the tragus forward and one can look right into the ear canal like a hole in the head—yet another stigma.

Layers: Most people think of a face-lift as simply tightening the skin. In the early days, that was the case. In fact, until recently, some of the most prominent plastic surgeons simply would remove a strip of skin in front of the ear and close it. This thirty-minute procedure still has some supporters amongst those who like their patients to come back every two years for another one. They even justify it by claiming that it's the little nips and tucks that make aging stand still and that the patient never looks different. In reality, these little procedures only serve to gradually stretch the skin, eventually creating a very odd appearance.

To really create a smooth, natural contour, more than the skin has to be altered. There is a layer beneath the skin composed of muscle, fascia, and fat, with the acronym SMAS (subcutaneous musculo-aponeurotic system), which usually needs to be tightened as separate layer. A good analogy is found in the art of bed-making. There's a bedsheet with a blanket over it; however, if you don't first smooth the wrinkles in the sheet, the blanket will never be smooth, no matter how tightly you pull it or how great your hospital corners are.

Tightening the SMAS moves some of the facial fat back into a more youthful position and takes up most of the slack, permitting the skin to be redraped over the newly tightened framework without tension. It heals better and looks more natural, and I believe it lasts longer, too. (I say "I believe" because scientifically measured results are very hard to come by with aesthetic surgery.)

Strange as it may seem, it often takes *more* of a procedure to get a result that looks *less* altered.

Repositioning of fat: Fat has a bad rap. "Fat-free" or "Low-fat" claims fly off food wrappers. In fact, without a nice even layer of fat beneath the skin and above the muscle, the softness and natural appearance of the face would be gone. If you have ever seen someone unfortunate enough to have had a large skin graft to the face—perhaps for a burn—you know what I mean. The graft attaches directly to the muscle, with no intervening fat layer. It is fat that makes the softness of a beautiful face. Without fat, it would look skeletal.

Repositioning the SMAS layer helps restore the fatty contours under the skin. In other cases, naturally-occurring fat pads are suspended with sutures. And many times, fat is taken from elsewhere on the body and injected into the face to fill it out. (An ideological war has been developing in our ranks between those who feel that tissues should be lifted and tightened, and those who think that fat should be injected and no tightening should be done at all. It makes for interesting debates, but in fact, most reasonable surgeons know that the truth is somewhere in between the two extremes.)

Adequate undermining: Back to the bedsheet analogy. Try to smooth out either the top sheet or the blanket with someone sitting in the middle of the bed. Not exactly a smooth result. You have to release the attachments (or kick the person off the bed) to make it even. This requires that the facial skin and the SMAS layer be undermined widely and separated from underlying attachments so that they can be repositioned smoothly.

All of these are inherent in modern face-lift techniques, but there is another, even more basic aspect to creating a good face-lift: the ease and skill of the operating surgeon, the way in which he or she treats the patient's tissues. Ask any operating room nurse who has been around for a few years about the difference between surgeons. You will always hear two adjectives mentioned: *smooth* and *rough*. A smooth surgeon moves easily, purposefully, and gently, treating the tissues in a delicate manner. A rough one struggles, sweats, sometime throws tantrums and instruments, and abuses the tissues mercilessly. At the end of the day, the smoother surgeon will inevitably produce less bruising, less complications, and quicker healing than the rough one, even if they have technically done exactly the same procedure.

Another issue that is rarely discussed in training is the number of times a patient can have a face-lift without looking too "plastic." Although there is no absolute number, I find that three is about all the face-lifts a person can carry off and still look reasonably normal. After that, one starts to run out of hair in which to hide the scars, and there is a definite danger of looking too "pulled." Some patients are compulsively driven to repeated surgeries to avoid any vestige of aging, and there is usually a surgeon somewhere ready to come to their aid.

But before we summarily scorn the surgeon for pandering to a neurotically needy patient, it's necessary to look at the picture from another side. Not all patients seem to mind that "stretched-out" result that many of us find distasteful. Inevitably, we are faced with hopeful patients in their seventies and eighties who want "one last face-lift." They already show the signs of too much surgery, but when they look in the mirror, all they see is loose tissues that make them feel aged.

It's very easy to pontificate about excessive surgery, which I tend to do incessantly, but in the end, it is up to the surgeon to decide how to handle the situation. Should he stick to his aesthetic principles and tell the patient enough is enough? Or should he acknowledge that not everyone lives according to his taste and do the procedure, which in all likelihood will make the patient very happy? Not an easy choice.

❖ Complications

Hematomas are the most common complications in any surgery, including face-lifts. Surgeons take great precautions to avoid them, and they are rare; yet they still occur. We check lab tests preoperatively to make sure there are no clotting problems that might cause bleeding. During surgery, we are extremely careful to cauterize even the minutest blood vessel, and postoperatively, we have a supportive dressing. Until recently, I used drains (small tubes with holes in them) to keep fluid suctioned out from beneath the skin flaps, but for the past three years, I've used tissue glue to seal the tissue planes together. Despite all the precautions, postoperative hematoma is still the most common complication. That said, it occurs in way less than 1 percent of my patients.

❖ Conjugal Convalescence

Minnie B was an old friend, a gentle, smiling, pretty blonde, originally from Arkansas, but now she harkened from Ketchum, Idaho. She gave an aura of being a totally complete person at one with herself and with the world. Her husband, Tom, was similarly kindly, uncomplicated, and very attentive to Minnie.

She had a face-lift on a Monday, and everything went smoothly. Nowadays, I send all my patients to an aftercare facility where nurses look after them in a supportive and experienced manner. But in those days, Minnie and Tom wanted to save the money, so they were staying in a nearby motel. I saw her the morning after the operation and changed the bandages, and all was perfectly fine. There was minimal pain and swelling, and there was no sign of bruising. I told them to come back in two more days to have the dressings removed and some of the sutures taken out.

At about 1:00 AM on Wednesday, I received a call from a very worried-sounding Tom. He said that the left side of Minnie's face was swollen, painful, and bruised. I knew instantly from his description that this was a hematoma, so I called in the OR crew with apologies for disturbing their sleep, and we all met at the office. Minnie did indeed have a large hematoma, and I needed to take her back to surgery and remove the clotted blood and cauterize any bleeding blood vessels that caused it.

Before we went into the OR, I asked Minnie what had happened prior to the onset of the swelling, seeing that she had been doing so well prior to that.

She started, "Well, Tom and I were making love and—"

"Making love?" I said incredulously. "Minnie, you know I said no sex for about two weeks after surgery."

She replied sheepishly, "I forgot about that, but anyway, nothing went wrong when we did it last night."

Minnie and Tom had managed to sneak in a little romance the night immediately following the surgery. They got away with it, so they thought they would try it again. Since that time, I make my instructions more explicit: For the first two weeks, no sex, no exercise, no sports, and no operating heavy equipment, whatever that means.

The most feared complication—fortunately a very rare one—is permanent injury to a motor nerve. This can be manifest as a drooping eyebrow, a crooked smile, or most commonly, a weakness of the muscle that pulls the corner of the mouth downward on animation. Although I have seen a very few, very memorable nerve weaknesses in my practice, I have been fortunate in not ever seeing a permanent one, but sometimes the temporary ones can be quite worrisome.

A few years ago, I did a face-lift on a woman TV news reporter from a large Midwestern city. Everything seemed to go very well, but in the first few days after her surgery, it became apparent that she had an injury to the left ramus mandibularis nerve, the nerve that innervates the corner of the mouth. This is the most frequently injured of all the facial nerves. Upon speaking or animation, the right side moved properly, but the left corner of the lower lip would not pull downward as desired. I reassured her that this would probably be temporary. (I reassured *her*, but what about me? I was worried that maybe somehow I had permanently injured the nerve during the dissection under the jawbone.)

My anxiety grew as the first week went by. She was healing beautifully, and in another two weeks, she would be home and on camera reporting the news. I couldn't have her looking like something had gone wrong. When the end of the second week had arrived and the left corner of the mouth still wouldn't move downward, I felt something needed to be done so that she could go back to work and not show any problems.

Inability to pull down the corner of the mouth is only obvious to an onlooker when it is one-sided. Clever problem solver that I am, I injected a small amount of Botox into the uninjured muscle on the other side of the face, thus weakening that side in a like manner. The result was a symmetrical mouth that moved evenly. The Botox would last about six weeks, which would be enough time to ensure that the left side would be healed, if it were ever going to, that is. And home she went back to her home and the evening news.

It was a very clever solution. Except that two days after she got home, the left-side weakness that I was focused on disappeared completely, and then she was stuck with the Botox-weakened right side. The solution? Another injection of Botox—this time in the left side. Problem solved!

While the type and extent of the surgery may be defined by the anatomy and the condition of the patient's face, there is much more to it than that. A good doctor also takes into consideration the patient's personality, lifestyle, and mind-set. A well-known actress may need more aggressive facial treatment in order to project a youthful appearance on camera than a business professional who wants to look better—refreshed, alert, and younger—in a way that his or her colleagues can't quite pinpoint.

Even with actresses, it is a balancing act, and you must know exactly where the balance is. I had repeatedly held off operating on a famous TV star who was anxious for a second face-lift. I didn't want her to end up looking "overdone" rather than well done. But finally, ten years after her first face-lift, she exclaimed in exasperation, "They're making me wear those 'lifts' now when I'm on camera." (Lifts are pieces of clear tape attached to the cheeks in front of the ear and to the upper neck just below the earlobe, which are then pulled by elastic bands over and behind the head. The elastics are usually covered by a wig. The apparatus tends to be quite uncomfortable.) I took a long hard look at her face and decided it was time. The surgery was a smashing success. No more lifts, and she's looking forward to another ten years of professional longevity in the same role.

From a "minilift" requiring no more than a lifting of the skin of the cheeks to an entire overhaul that includes a brow lift, eyelids, and a chin implant, a patient must have the information he or she needs to help make decisions about the specific procedures that are right for him or her. For instance, an older patient who has had a prior face-lift may only need a partial lift to improve the appearance. By contrast, a younger man or woman with mild to moderate signs of aging might look incredible with a much more extensive procedure yet still appear as if nothing had been done at all. This may seem contradictory, but it works.

Over the years, I have noticed that the patients who come to me for face-lifts are often experiencing certain landmark events in their lives. In no particular order, they include an upcoming high school reunion, the wedding of a child, the completion of divorce proceedings (sometimes the very instant that the much-maligned ex moves out), and even the death of a loved one.

In the last case, it's essential that surgery wait until emotional healing has occurred. While I know how buoying an emotional lift is at these moments—and a good face-lift can provide a huge confidence boost—it is not necessarily the time for elective surgery. Not only can the healing process be compromised by stress or sorrow, but it is very important that a patient be in a stable emotional place to be able to withstand both the physical and psychological changes inherent in any cosmetic surgery procedure.

CHAPTER SEVEN
WHEN IS TOO MUCH NOT ENOUGH?

Your lips like bratwursts,
Your breasts like casabas,
Your eyes like Cleopatra's cat,
Your face tight and immobile as death.
What happened to my beloved?

—Anonymous

In Beverly Hills, as in many upscale communities around the world, unfortunate victims of excessive plastic surgery are seen all too commonly walking along the street, in fashionable restaurants, in the VIP zones of premieres and benefits, in the local supermarket. If we live in more rural areas, we find them in the popular media, TV, the tabloids. But wherever they are seen, the reaction is the same: Why would anyone do that to themselves? Is it just a matter of poor taste? Is a more deeply seated emotional conflict to blame?

To some degree, my Midwestern upbringing has protected me from the influence of daily exposure to over-operated, body-dysmorphic denizens of southern California. If it taught me to believe in anything, it is that true beauty comes from within. Its visual manifestation must remain within the scale of normal human appearances. When it stretches beyond the realm of normalcy, it may be interesting or bizarre or maybe even sexy, *but it is not beautiful.*

If you ask any plastic surgeon, he or she would never admit that they deliberately do "too much." There is an easy kind of lip service among physicians that a plastic surgical procedure must be performed *appropriately* on a patient with reasonable expectations, without the plastic-look similes: "deer-in-the-headlights" or "too much time on the back of a motorcycle" or "porn-star boobs."

Then how do you explain the late great Michael Jackson's nose, Pamela Anderson's breasts, or perhaps the queen of it all, Jocelyn Wildenstein's everything? Who is doing these procedures if all the doctors claim they wouldn't participate in such wretched excess? And why?

One reason is that very important people—celebrities, titans of industry, billionaires—have, for all their advantages, one serious disadvantage: they never hear the word *no.* Or if they do, they are so unsatisfied with it that they change it to *yes.* In the case of plastic surgery, if a physician has the good taste and integrity to refuse to operate on one of these patients, it is a certainty that some doctor next door or around the block will say, "Absolutely! When would you like to begin?"

And sometimes, the physician whose better judgment prods him to demur, may acknowledge the fact that he ought to do the procedure anyway. After all, if he doesn't do it, the patient will inevitably find another surgeon, almost certainly of lesser moral fiber and surgical skill. Acting in what is perceived as the patient's best interest, he makes the nose narrower, the breasts larger, the face tighter, the lips bigger, the eyes more catlike. In short, he creates exactly that which he would publicly denounce.

My wife has an interesting theory about Prince Charles: he must have been a lousy lover. (She categorically denies any firsthand knowledge.) Why? Because prowess in making love, like many other skills, grows from learning through experience. His early experiences in that sphere probably led him to believe that no matter what he did or didn't do, he was indeed the world's greatest living lover. How many young women would ever tell him, "Um, excuse me, Your Royal Highness. That's just not doing anything for me"? A possible answer: about the same number of plastic surgeons that said *no* to Michael Jackson.

In regard to the difficulty of saying *no*, Dr. Gurdin would often warn me, "Norm, I'd rather have a patient angry with me for saying no than have them angry with me for operating on them."

In fact, I have found that when I feel surgery is not the right choice for a particular patient at this particular time, not only are they not angry, but they are grateful. Many times, they have felt pressure to have plastic surgery for reasons with which they're not completely comfortable, and my refusal is a huge relief for them. Others, of course, will quickly look to the surgeon across the street.

Even when they are disappointed, they respect me for my honesty. It is sadly too common that I see a patient whom I have turned away years ago come back to me after they've had their operation elsewhere with unfortunate and possibly irreparable results. The satisfaction I get from knowing that my prior decisions were sound doesn't reduce my empathy for these unfortunate patients.

The risk of saying no is compounded by the knowledge that plastic surgery has become a very competitive business.

❖ Be Careful What You Wish For

Much of my professional life is involved in the world of actors and actresses, where the line between fantasy and reality is very blurry. Working actors (as opposed to the much more populous group of *aspiring* actors) are constantly exposed to their own appearances. They see their made-up, coiffed, professionally lit faces frozen in time in feature films, TV shows, and series with endless reruns (if they're lucky), and then they look in the mirror and see the actual thing. And their reflection tells them that time is not in fact standing still.

Actors in general tend to be more insecure than the average person. They know that their continued success depends upon their appeal to their viewers or fans, but of even more immediate concern, they need to get hired for a job or keep an ongoing part in a series. This is most difficult for women. A successful young actress will have her choice of scripts, but as she ages, she might find that her choices aren't quite so vast. Eventually, she may actually have to go and read (audition) for a part that she would have turned down a few years earlier.

There are exceptions, of course. Meryl Streep puts in a spectacular performance on a yearly basis, and it seems her versatility is boundless. Katharine Hepburn aged "gracefully" and worked as long as she desired. But both of these talented actresses are anomalies in the business. Most leading ladies know that younger, prettier actresses are lining up right behind them, and keeping up their appearance is the key to continued success.

"I can't play the ingénue anymore."

"They only want me to play the mother."

It is easier for male actors. They may be permitted to age gracefully, but they need to maintain an aura of vitality, virility, and perhaps most of all, integrity in order to be hirable.

"The director says I look tired."

"The lighting guy says he can't light me anymore because of these bags under my eyes."

These are among the chief complaints that many actors present to me when seeking plastic surgery consultation. And within the framework of their work, they may be completely valid. My problem is that I might not be able to provide enough of an improvement to make it worthwhile—worth their scars, their risks, their pain, their money. Even though they are desperate for the aesthetic "boost" they seek, I sometimes have to tell them to wait.

Most listen. Some don't. Some will go so far to attempt to ensure their continued success that they create the very thing they fear the most—a loss of the features that made them desirable in the first place. And in these cases, their celebrity works to their disadvantage. It's very hard to say *no* to a really famous person, and unfortunately, *no* is what they often need to hear.

There's a story circulating around Hollywood about Alfonso Bedoya, the great Mexican character actor, who was most famous for his role in the classic John Huston film *The Treasure of the Sierra Madre*. His lined, weather-beaten face, craggy features, and crooked teeth helped him create a character of unforgettable badness. His famous line "We don't have to show you no steenkin' badges!" is right up there with "Here's lookin' at you, kid," "Frankly, my dear, I don't give a damn," and "Go ahead, make my day!"

Alfonso Bedoya worked regularly and became very famous. And then, for whatever reason—maybe he was concerned about losing his status to a younger, better-looking actor—it's said that he had everything "fixed": his teeth, his lines, his nose. And he never acted again.

Some biographers say he drank himself to death. His career as a character actor relied upon his appearance of anything but the classic sense of beauty. The art of plastic surgery was not up to the task of improving his appearance while preserving those unique features. It wasn't in the '50s, and it isn't today. It probably will never be, because no one wants to see a smooth, unlined, handsome Alfonso Bedoya. We will always remember him as the rugged *bandito* and not as the stereotypic ranch hand buffoon of his last movie, *The Big Country*, with few wrinkles and straight teeth, even if one of them was gold.

I have stated that most of my patients are not performers and that even superstars have the same anatomy and anxieties as regular folks, but I will admit to a little thrill in seeing one of my patients receiving the ultimate awards for their craft—the Oscar, the Tony, the Emmy, the Grammy. I know that my work has nothing *directly* to do with their achievement, yet I feel a sense of pride by association.

Plastic surgery definitely can have major effects on the careers of performers, either for better or for worse. It is the rule that most sexy leading ladies have had breast surgery, either augmentation or lifting, sometimes both. I will further state without fear of contradiction that most actors or actresses over the age of forty-five have had some plastic surgery, most commonly blepharoplasty (eyelids) or a face-lift.

If the surgery has been done well, it will improve the appearance needed to initiate interest on the part of jaded casting agents and producers. Perhaps more importantly, the surgery will enhance the self-confidence required by a performer whose only power is that which they can create with their attitude, their voice, and their posture. If the surgery has been done poorly, exactly the opposite will occur. The responsibility is significant.

There is a more subtle aspect to what makes a plastic surgery procedure successful in a famed celebrities—namely its appropriateness. In the example of Alfonso Bedoya as in the tragic case of Michael Jackson, the work was doomed to fail because the goals were completely inappropriate. Not enough surgeons said *no* to them. Everyone who has watched the Academy Awards regularly sees famed actors and actresses with surgical results that imply adequate technique (at best) but totally insensitive goals. We like our rugged men to look rugged, not surprised or beady-eyed. And we don't want our Audrey Hepburns looking like Pamela Andersons.

There are certain anatomic features that are symbolic of youth, beauty, femininity, or masculinity. The ease by which these features can be surgically altered today opened the gates to deeply ingrained fantasies. Breasts have always been symbols of fertility and sexuality.

Now that breast implants are so readily available, women can have the breasts they previously could only dream about. Most just want fuller breasts to feel more feminine, but some women want huge porn-star breasts. Some actually are porn stars.

In another area, soft, plump lips are archetypal of a feminine, youthful beauty. Huge, bulky lips are the perverted extension of that desire. Men also want to look younger and more masculine, but they may end up with chins and pecs that jut out like shelves. And yes, some people even want Michael's nose. Go figure. It's odd that some admirers will do whatever they can to look like a certain celebrity no matter how bizarre he or she might appear.

But why? What is it that would move a moderately intelligent, well-integrated person to want to change his or her appearance in such a dramatic and blatantly artificial manner? Did they just start out wanting some improvement and go overboard? Do they really think that they would look better with such an obvious distortion of reality? Or are they simply a product of a possibly well-trained (or not) plastic surgeon whose surgical abilities overwhelm his sense of propriety and taste?

This last point is a thorny one. I have participated in the training of plastic surgery residents at UCLA for the past thirty years. I have seen many of them go through the program, take their board exams, and go into the world.

Some have stayed in an academic program doing basic research, performing more and more amazing reconstructive procedures, and running residency programs at universities across the United States. Others have gone into private or group practices, focusing exclusively on aesthetic surgery. Still others maintain a "balanced" practice, struggling through long nights of emergency trauma cases, doing their cosmetic cases part of the time, and maintaining a teaching position part-time.

But whatever the path they choose, they all have completed a training program that has taught them a great deal about the anatomy and physiology of human tissues. What it may not have taught them is that which is the hardest to teach. Some have called it a *sense of aesthetics*, and others have referred to it as *an eye*.

I call it *taste*.

I know of many surgeons who are highly skilled and can perform wondrous feats of surgical virtuosity. But some of these surgeons simply cannot perform a face-lift without creating a completely artificial appearance. Patients desiring a cosmetic procedure don't really care if the doctor is a genius with burns, head and neck cancer reconstruction, or hand surgery, although these are highly prized qualities within those arenas. What the usual cosmetic surgery patient hopes for is a natural-appearing improvement, one that evokes positive, ego-boosting comments from onlookers but one whose tracks are invisible. That is the goal, and to achieve that requires both skill *and* taste in substantial quantities.

Other times, a patient's overdone appearance stems from a perverse persistence to achieve a fantasized perfection. Body dysmorphic syndrome is a condition marked by severely distorted self-image. An anorexic person may feel they are fat when the whole world can see that they are emaciated. Similarly, BDS patients see the slightest physical imperfection as a hideous deformity, and they constantly seek an elusive and inevitably hazardous correction.

It's common for an adolescent girl going on a first date to see a small pimple as a completely disabling freakish disaster, but having raised such an individual, I know that this is the norm for behavior under those circumstances. This is not BDS, just normal teenage neurotic behavior.

I hope.

BDS is a much more serious distortion of perception, occurring in adults as well as adolescents. Many such patients find their way to the plastic surgeon's office, seeking a surgical answer to an unsolvable problem. If a plastic surgeon is unwise or unlucky enough to operate upon such a patient, he may end up paying for his ill-advised decision with his peace of mind, his reputation, his malpractice insurance, and in some cases, his life. Sadly, there have been more than a few highly publicized incidents of plastic surgeons having been killed by deranged, usually BDS patients.

Most of the bizarre people we see with extremely artificial appearances suffer from at least a touch of BDS. They inevitably blame their previous plastic surgeon(s) for their appearance, and yet they seek out more. Like most psychological conditions, there is a wide range to the affliction. These individuals range from those who are just a little more finicky than the usual to the completely out-of-touch lunatic who not only wants to look like Elvis but *be* Elvis. The extreme expression of the disorder is easy to spot and avoid, but even the most experienced surgeon can sometimes be taken unaware and inevitably live to regret it.

❖ *Mrs. Wong from Hong Kong*

Mike Gurdin used to say that the best patients were from out of town. "They have their surgery, pay their bill, and go back home." Of course, Mike practiced in the Golden Age of Medicine, before aggressive malpractice lawyers, daily jumbo jet flights anywhere in the world, and e-mail. Times have most definitely changed.

I had received an urgent call on a Thursday from a woman who had just arrived in Los Angeles from Hong Kong, literally halfway around the world. She told Suzanne, my office manager, that she was only here for one week, and she desperately needed to have her upper lids fixed. I told Suzanne to work her in for consultation the next day, being quite flattered that she had heard of my reputation from so far away and that she had made the trip just to see me.

I missed the first red flag: Watch out for a patient who flatters excessively. You are the best. You are the only one who can help her.

She just flew in from Neptune to see only you. Inevitably, it is bait, and you ought to be very concerned lest you get hooked.

That Friday morning, Mrs. Wong explained in a rather tense and hurried fashion that she had had her eyelids hideously deformed by a plastic surgeon in Korea. Further questioning brought out the fact that she had also had her eyelids hideously deformed by plastic surgeons in Hong Kong, in Tokyo, and in Singapore.

"Please," she said. "You must help me." She was a prominent socialite in Hong Kong, and she had not been able to attend any society functions for the last year because of her deformity. As if to emphasize the importance of her plight, she added that she drove a Rolls-Royce.

Another missed red flag: When a patient reports that all the other surgeons are incompetent boobs (in so many words) but she knows that you will save her, be very careful, for this is a heavy escalation of the flattery warning. Also, seriously, there are more Rolls-Royces than Chevrolets in Beverly Hills.

I examined her hideously deformed upper lids and saw, as I expected, nothing really bad, only a slightly more prominent scar than usual—no hideousness. In fact, they looked pretty good. I saw the whole scenario, and then as experienced as I was and armed against the pitfalls that "lesser" plastic surgeons may fall into, I fell for it.

"This is really an incredibly easy case," I rationalized. "It's simply an upper lid scar revision. I can easily improve it, and she'll be back home in Hong Kong before she knows it."

I forcibly ignored the little Jiminy Cricket conscience sitting on my shoulder that softly whispered, "You'll be sorry."

I took her on as a patient, did a simple, neat twenty-minute procedure, and then it all began … in the recovery room. Barely awake from the brief anesthetic, she demanded a hand mirror and then began to wail loudly that I had destroyed her face. She was inconsolable, and after one hour of explanation, of reassurance that what she saw at the moment was completely unrelated to the eventual result (although she looked perfectly fine to me), we managed to get her into the car for the trip to the aftercare facility.

The sound of my palm smacking my forehead could be heard all the way to the Great Wall. How dumb could I have been to ignore all the warnings I knew so well? It was too late for regrets now. She was now my patient, and I was her doctor.

The next few days were a nightmare of tap dancing, explaining how healing takes a little time, how I had barely done anything, and how she would look so much better when she returned home, which, I suggested, should be as soon as possible. She finally went back to Hong Kong, and I, along with my staff, breathed a sigh of relief. It was over.

The faxes started to arrive about one week later. They arrived daily and then several times a day, each more and more menacing. They were long, handwritten, angry tirades. I began to have bad dreams involving a ninja gang (I know, they're Japanese, but hey, it was a dream) would appear in my home, exacting cruel and horrifying vengeance upon me and my family.

The frequency of the faxes slowly simmered down to one every few days. Then one day about three months later, she appeared unannounced in my office (looking fine) and told me that she wanted some financial recompense for her suffering. She said that she had not been out of her house since her surgery, that she was deformed beyond recognition, and that she was becoming the laughing stock of her mah-jongg club.

I examined her face carefully. Her lids looked perfectly fine, and the scars of the upper lids were in fact much less noticeable than before her ill-advised surgery. However, in order to peacefully and rapidly resolve the situation, I offered to give her back her surgical fee and expenses: $2,500. Problem solved.

She said that would not be adequate. She had required two round-trip, first-class Cathay Pacific tickets (the first trip for the surgery, the second for the negotiations, both unsolicited), plus two weeks stay in a bungalow at the Beverly Hills Hotel, plus some compensation for her pain. It was clear that Mrs. Wong had been reading up on the American system of justice.

She demanded $60,000.

I knew that there had been no negligence, that her result was excellent, and that no malpractice attorney in his or her right mind would take this case, but I preferred to end it peacefully and say good-bye rather than fight an endlessly tiring battle. I offered her a good faith settlement of $5,000, knowing that I was better off settling than wearing myself out fighting her.

Her response: $50,000.

Nathan Road. It came back to me in a flash. I am a battle-weary veteran of shopping and haggling experiences in jewelry stores on Nathan Road in Kowloon with my wife, and the similarities became quickly apparent. I was determined not to play that game. I told her that $5,000 was my final offer, and she could accept it within twenty-four hours or it would be withdrawn. She refused but wanted to haggle on. I excused myself and left the room: I had other patients to attend to.

Twenty-four hours went by, and other than a brief phone call in which she said she would take $40,000, I heard nothing more. She left me with a letter saying that she would seek legal action against me and flew home.

After several months had elapsed, I had almost forgotten about her. One day nearly nine months after her surgery, I was in the middle of performing a breast reduction in my surgicenter when my secretary called in over the intercom.

"Dr. Leaf, *Mrs. Wong is here.*"

A few words that ruined my day. I told Chris that she should explain to Mrs. Wong that I wouldn't be able to speak to her until I was finished with the surgery and that she could come back in about two hours.

There was a silence, and then Chris called back in and said, "She says she won't leave until she speaks to you." She also indicated that Mrs. Wong was becoming abusive and disturbing other patients that were waiting to see my colleagues.

"Tell her to wait quietly, or you'll have to ask her to leave," I told Chris.

There was a slight pause before Chris continued, "Dr. Leaf, she won't leave, and she's beginning to break the place up. Should I call the police?"

This was an entirely new situation for me. I had heard about patients becoming violent. In fact, a fine plastic surgeon I knew in the Chicago area had just recently been shot and killed by a deranged patient.

"Call the police," I said and resumed concentrating on my surgery patient. After a ten-minute pause, Chris called in and said, "I think you'd better come out here, Dr. Leaf."

I felt I had wasted enough energy already, and I told Chris that I would be there when I was finished.

"You'd better come out here now, sir," she replied. Her voice was low, and she sounded serious. Besides, she never had called me "sir" before. I broke scrub and went out of the OR to the front office. (Clarification: taking a break during surgery is not uncommon, nor is it dangerous.)

Mrs. Wong was lying facedown on the floor of the waiting room wailing pitifully, her wrists handcuffed behind her. Standing in front of me was a perspiring, red-faced, young Beverly Hills police officer writing something on a pad. He had a small cut on his lip. Apparently, my patient had slugged him in the face and kneed him in the groin, and he had wrestled her to the floor, cuffed her, and called for backup.

Mrs. Wong spotted me and cried out pathetically. "Dr. Leaf, please let me go!"

A plainclothes detective had now joined the scene, and I asked him quietly if he couldn't just release her, let her sit up, and talk in a more civilized manner. There were other patients in the waiting room, and I couldn't tell if they were horrified or fascinated by the action.

"This is out of your hands now, Doc," he said. "She assaulted a Beverly Hills police officer."

This was something like an old vaudeville act I had seen on TV about a man who spits on the subway and, through a process of hilarious legal bungles, winds up going to the electric chair.

I explained to the detective about what had built up to this encounter, and he took some notes and made a call to headquarters. After a moment or two, he came back with a solution that will forever endear me to the Beverly Hills police force. *Deus ex Machina* in blue.

"We're gonna escort her to LAX (Los Angeles International Airport) and make sure she's on the next plane for Hong Kong."

And the *coup de grace*: "And we're issuing a bench warrant for her arrest on a felony assault charge. If she ever sets foot in Beverly Hills again, she's goin' to jail."

A relief tinged with guilt: I knew that I had behaved far too moronically to deserve such a satisfying ending, but I happily went back to the operating room and never heard from Mrs. Wong again.

I got away easy.

Body dysmorphic disorder appears in varying degrees of pathology. Mrs. Wong was an example of a patient at the midlevel of dysfunction, more of a serious pain in the ass than anything else. The degree of dysfunction seems to be directly related to the degree of bizarre postsurgical appearance. Such patients wind up in much more serious trouble as a result of their pathological insistence on obtaining more and more plastic surgery from an ever-growing population of plastic surgeons willing to whip out their scalpels at the drop of a dime.

BDS aside, a few examples stand out and cry for inclusion in a "Top Ten List of Most Surgically Inappropriate Results." The few names I may mention are not my patients, so I'm not revealing any privileged medical details. I may have met them socially or in passing, but my observations are largely from the same source that the public has access to—the tabloids.

Without further ado, in reverse order of distortion, and with apologies to Dave Letterman, here are my nominations for my top ten horror stories:

❖ *Top Ten Worst Plastic Surgery Distortions*

#10. Too much filler.
Restylane, Juvederm, fat—*anything that can be done can and will be overdone.* The nasolabial fold is a case in point. These are the creases that go diagonally away from the side of the nose down toward the corner of the mouth. Everyone has them—kids, teenagers, Paris Hilton, everyone. People who are more expressive have more prominent ones. Fillers work well to reduce them, and they are very popular for that purpose. There comes a time when it would be more appropriate to do surgical lifting of the cheeks and jowls instead of just building the creases up, but some keep pumping them full of fillers, the result being a rounder, fatter face with no delineation. Still, it's less obvious than the next of the top ten.

#9. Too much Botox.

Although it's not technically a surgical procedure, Botox injections, like fillers or surgery, can be done well, overdone, or underdone. The most common problem with overdoing it is the appearance of a completely immobile, expressionless face. One obvious tip-off results from the attempt to eliminate the horizontal lines of the forehead. Those lines are caused by muscles that lift the eyebrows by contraction, and Botox acts by reducing the ability of that muscle to contract.

If the horizontal forehead lines are injected a bit too much, the muscles are weakened to the point that the eyebrows descend very low over the eyelids, and the only remnant of brow motion remains at the outer corners. When the patient attempts to look upward, the outer brows go up slightly and the result is very much like a high school depiction of the devil. *Look around, because you'll spot this in a flash.*

#8. Brow lifting.

The catlike brow elevation of Ms. Wildenstein is a classic case of overdoing it (see BDS). There was a time when plucking, teasing, and waxing of the brows was used (and abused) to create a sophisticated, open-eyed, seen-it-all attitude. Tattooing of brows in that position seemed like a good answer, but unless done with sensitivity to the aging process, they ultimately look bizarre and become permanent and virtually uncorrectable.

Surgical forehead/brow lifting is a wonderful procedure when it is done subtly. It positions the brows in a fresh, youthful position and makes the eyes appear alert and youthful. Unfortunately, some of the newer techniques are prone to over-elevation of the brows, and this is also somewhat permanent. There is a huge difference between bright, youthful eyes and the appearance of having just sat on a thumbtack. As I have said before, anything that can be done can be overdone.

#7. Cheekbones and chin implants.

There are a variety of silicone implants in different sizes and shapes made for the purpose of adding definition to the cheekbones or chin. The areas can also be filled out by other means, surgical and nonsurgical. More and more, we find that the desired definition can be achieved by shifting the patient's own soft tissues during a face-lift or midface-lift. Injectable fillers can also produce a fairly long-lasting roundness of the upper cheeks, a very rejuvenating look. In any case, the result should be a blunted prominence, not a sharp-edged, narrow flange or a skeletal appearance.

#6. Face peels and laser resurfacing.

Nothing works as effectively as these two modalities to eliminate deeply etched wrinkles and age spots. The outer layer of the skin is removed either by an acid (face peel) or by light energy (laser resurfacing). Both procedures can be very effective, but both are quite uncomfortable to experience, require a prolonged recovery, and tend to produce smooth "alabaster" facial skin with little if any skin pigment. The deeper the treatments go, the more lines and wrinkles are removed, but the flip side of alabaster is a ghostly paleness, which is not so attractive and may require constant makeup.

Despite these drawbacks, peeling and laser resurfacing are here to stay, and especially with the newer fractionated CO_2 lasers, the results can be excellent. As always, too much of a good thing is disastrous. The overly tight, almost skeletal faces of some of the entertainment industry's leading ladies and men stand as taut, silent examples of gratuitous overtreatment.

#5. Face-lifts.

Some celebrities have joked about their face-lifts with great success. Others have not but should. On camera, when they are all dolled up, they still may look pretty good. They may seem slightly "done" perhaps but not grotesquely so.

But what works for performers doesn't work so well for the rest of us. Up close and personal is a different viewpoint altogether. Too many plastic surgery victims seek to achieve that "entertainer" style appearance on their own real life faces and find doctors willing to follow their lead. You see them everywhere: taut stretched faces with "pull lines" on the cheeks, prominent scars around the ears, the earlobes pulled downward in a "pixie-ear" appearance, a stretched-out fish mouth, a plump round head on a thin neck ("pumpkin-on-a-stick"), and a complete lack of balance between the face and the rest of the body. Kindness prevents me from naming some of these obviously overdone celebrities, but you know who they are. For their sake, I hope they don't.

#4. Rhinoplasty.

Why is it that the worst results seem to occur in men? Men need to have a stronger nose to match their larger features. But even with a woman, when a nose is reduced too much, it doesn't balance the rest of the face. It also doesn't work very well. Let's not forget that a nose has a function other than holding up sunglasses. It has to be large enough inside to permit air to flow comfortably. Modern nasal surgery is directed toward achieving a well-defined nasal tip and bridge, and although the nose may be smaller than preoperatively, size alone is not the main concern. A proper rhinoplasty is as likely to have tissue added as well as taken away, and the best results look nothing at all like a pinched, pointy-tip, classic '60s nose job.

#3. Eyelids.

Most people think that a startled appearance is due to too much eyelid surgery. That can happen, but usually overzealous brow-lifting causes that unfortunate appearance. And again, most "bad" eyelid jobs are much worse in men. Most commonly that odd surgical look, the hound-dog sadness, results from overdoing the *lower* lids, but the excessive removal of upper lid skin is more dangerous. After all, we need our eyelids to close, don't we?

#2. Lips.

Thoughts might immediately fly to Angeline Jolie, Liv Tyler, or Scarlett Johannsen—women whom I believe have naturally full lips, at least to start with. These lips skirt the line between exceptional and abnormal, but they do so in a generally pleasing fashion. Also in this category are the actor Olivier Martinez and the late Jean-Paul Belmondo. *If anything at all* has been done to these lips (other than Belmondo, who died before collagen injections appeared), it is most likely the simple and temporary process of "plumping up" with Restylane or other fillers. This is basically an injection of an FDA-approved, biologically acceptable goo that may last from two to six months before it is gradually absorbed.

The FDA has not actually approved the substances for "plumping" the lips, but it has approved them for filling in the lines around the lips. The widely accepted "off-label" application of injecting into the lip itself is a small but significant step. Injecting one's own fat is also popular, perhaps longer-lasting but also a bit dicier. Fat injections are unpredictable in their longevity. In any case, the border between tempting lips and sausage lips is vague at best, but we know it when we see someone who has crossed it. The hilarious episode with Goldie Hawn and Rob Reiner in the comedy film *The First Wives Club* is an unforgettable send-up of that problem, which isn't so funny in real life.

Although many of these procedures have been largely abandoned, now and again I see a patient whose lips have been forever ruined by ill-advised surgical procedures. Be very, very careful. Operations that seem so simple and reasonable have a way of going very, very badly. Perhaps the most disfiguring one is trying to enhance the lips by removing a narrow strip of skin just above the upper lip. When the resultant wound is closed with sutures, the red part of the lip moves upward a little and appears "fuller." The resultant permanent deformity requires constant camouflage with lipstick or tattooing of pigment, and neither of these remedies can replace the loss of the tiny "white roll" that is an essential anatomic landmark between the lip and the skin above it.

Implantation of foreign, nonbiological substances like Gore-tex has become quite popular; this procedure is embraced mostly by physicians without real surgical training, such as dermatologists. It is a fairly easy, local anesthetic, office-type of procedure. Gore-tex, widely used in ski parkas, is also used very successfully in aortic surgery, and Gore-tex sutures are well-tolerated in many different operations; however, the implantation of a strip or a tiny tube of this material in the lips frequently produces a stiffness, a decrease in mobility in an area that must remain soft, pliable, and readily mobile. Although your lips may look good in still photographs, they just won't "look right" in real life, and they definitely won't pass the "kiss test," something not usually administered by the physician.

And extending this list below the face to its logical conclusion, the number one most surgically distorted feature is …

#1. Breasts, of course! (See *Are Those Real?*)

Let's face it: naturally large breasts do not stand straight out like apples or cantaloupes. Obeying the laws of gravity on soft structures, large, heavy breasts tend to hang or droop perhaps. And we can fix that, but making them smaller and higher is not what this item is about. This is about the *excesses* of plastic surgery, and nowhere have the excesses been more flaunted than with the surgical augmentation of the female breast.

Pamela Anderson has made no secret of her up-and-down-and-up-again bosom configuration. And no matter what, it works for her. It's a question of attitude and image. She shows her larger-than-life bosom with enthusiasm, and it's hard not to notice. She's not trying to "look normal." There's already enough of that in our world of reality. The same happened with Dolly Parton, who showed a little more humor and discretion but could carry off her "look" with grace and wit. And let's not ignore the incredibly lucrative porn industry, replete with industrial-sized breast implants. I'm actually surprised that we haven't yet seen an actress in an adult movie with *three* huge breasts (we haven't, have we?)—not just quality, but quantity, too.

Of course, in entertainers, we expect some degree of over-the-top appearance. The bizarre is commonplace, and entertainers get paid to be noticed. The big screen, the Country Music Awards, the red carpet at the Oscars—we expect our stars' bosoms to shine, jiggle, and heave. But as I mentioned before, life in the real world has a funny way of imitating art, a reversal from the traditional relationship. So it is that we see a woman's enormous breasts preceding her around a corner by a few seconds, not in some hip night spot but in the produce department of the local supermarket. It's hard not to stare more out of incredulity than admiration or lust. And staring, which translates to profitable bookings for performers, also produces ego boosts in the grocery shopper, a no less important benefit.

Will the time ever arrive when the indisputable silliness of such wretched excess becomes acceptable?

Has it already?

Is there a remedy for a culture obsessed with the impossibly overdone appearance?

Am I hypocritical by earning a living doing this work and then raising these questions?

And why am I asking *you* these questions? If I don't know the answer, who does?

As long as patients are willing to subject themselves to a surgical procedure to achieve an unnaturally altered state of existence and as long as there are surgeons willing to accommodate these inappropriate requests and give those patients *much more* of something than nature could ever bestow, then the process will continue. It isn't illegal, and as far as we can tell, it isn't harmful to their health.

It's just *bad taste,* and it's unlikely that will ever go out of style.

CHAPTER EIGHT
NOT JUST A PRETTY FACE

There is one side of plastic surgery that's rarely shown in the tabloids, simply because it doesn't have the gossipy excitement and glamorous aura of cosmetic surgery. That quiet, workaday aspect is *reconstruction* after major or minor trauma. Within the boundaries of our specialty as defined by the American Board of Plastic Surgery, reconstructive procedures actually outnumber cosmetic ones by a substantial margin.

The Los Angeles freeways provide an unending supply of severe injuries, the worst being those involving car vs. motorcycle. (Guess who inevitably loses that battle.) Gang violence in South Central LA, as on the south side of Chicago, runs the gamut from fistfights to stabbings all the way to unholy slaughters by automatic weapons. Children's playground injuries, kitchen mishaps, and the occasional dog bite round out the usual offerings from an urban practice. Still, there's a whole sphere of traumatic wounds with which I've had absolutely no experience until recently—military combat-induced wounds.

Our country is engaged in two wars today. Both these conflicts have produced horrifying injuries, most commonly resulting from a new type of weapon: the improvised explosive device (IED), also referred to as the "roadside bomb." Oddly enough, even though I practice cosmetic surgery in Beverly Hills I find myself very involved in the care of these wounded warriors.

These wars have been going on for well over five years, and our casualties are approaching six thousand. During a lesser length of time in the Vietnam War, we lost over fifty thousand American soldiers and marines. The reason for the substantial decrease in mortality is not a less determined or weaker enemy, but rather quantum-leap advances in immediate treatment of trauma. A large part of that is the near-instant medical emergency care and the rapid evacuation to acute care military treatment hospitals in Landstuhl Regional Medical Center, Germany. From there, stabilized patients are safely transported to Walter Reed, the Naval Hospital in Bethesda, Maryland, and Brooke Army Medical Center in Texas.

There is, however, a flip side to this reduced death rate. Those whose lives have been saved are returning home with heartbreaking, debilitating deformities of varying types and magnitudes. The worst injuries are not even visible: traumatic brain injuries. These brave men and women suffer in their own inarticulate universe, from which their loved ones are painfully excluded.

The veterans with amputated limbs are the ones most of us think about when we think about our wounded warriors, because they are exploited by the media as a source of great sound bites on the evening news. Even though they will usually be able to walk again with the help of modern prosthetic legs, their daily struggles to overcome their adversities are not to be trivialized. Amputated arms are much more difficult to deal with. Imagine trying to pick up a drink in a paper cup with an articulating hook device. Without sensory feedback, it's impossible to know how tightly one is squeezing the cup.

Then there are the multitudes of other deformities, major and minor, which might not be severe enough to warrant treatment through the Veterans Administration but could be helped substantially by modern reconstructive plastic surgery. In these cases, each veteran and his or her family must be their own advocate if they hope to get help with deforming scars of the face, loss of an eye or a nose or an ear, or significant problems with their arms, legs, hands, or feet.

Iraq Star Foundation is the brainchild of Maggie Lockridge, a nurse I've known for about twenty-five years. She was the first person to create the concept of the "aftercare facility" for post-op aesthetic surgery patients in the Beverly Hills area. This is essentially a means for recently operated patients to receive nursing care, medications, transportation, and meals in a posh hotel room near their doctors' offices and/or surgicenters. She started it as *Le Petit Ermitage* and continued with it through its different incarnations as hotels changed ownership or raised their rates. Maggie worked with many of my plastic surgery colleagues and ran her business smoothly and creatively, providing a nurturing and luxurious environment to ease our patients through their early recovery.

She recently retired, and befitting a woman who cannot stand idleness, she came up with a wonderful new idea that she could once again use to help patients recover. This time, however, the patients were our military troops, and the recovery was not from face-lifts or breast surgery but from wounds created by IEDs, land mines, suicide bombers, RPGs (rocket-propelled grenades), and the lethal shrapnel from any of these antipersonnel weapons.

What I didn't know about Maggie until recently was that long before she took care of my face-lift patients, she had been a U.S. Air Force nurse during the Vietnam War. I was a surgery resident at that time, and both Maggie and I recalled the bitter reception that our veterans experienced upon their return. America was going through enormous social and emotional upheavals at that time, and the national anger at that seemingly useless war had spilled over onto the backs of our veterans. They became pariahs in their own country. When Maggie saw television reportage of returning Iraq War vets coming home with crippling deformities, she was determined that they would not received the same sort of second-class treatment that prevailed forty years earlier.

The worthiness or wastefulness of these wars is a non-issue when one is involved in treating the suffering and deformities that our combat troops have sustained. (Personally, I feel that our initial response to 9/11 in Afghanistan was justified, but subsequently we were led into a war in Iraq that will never be justified. Maggie and I don't always agree on things like that, so we keep politics out of our discussions.)

Our veterans have served their country bravely and well. They were (and are) our children, our brothers and sisters, our young parents, all placed in harm's way in a distant, hostile land. When they return home with injuries, we owe them more than an honorable discharge. They deserve our gratitude and our support. They are young men and women who are looking forward to their future. They want jobs, careers, and education. They want to date, fall in love, and reenter society on equal footing with their uninjured peers, but a disfiguring scar, a missing facial feature, or even a significantly distorted smile can interfere with all those hopes.

Maggie called me one day in the spring of 2007 and asked if I'd help recruit some of my colleagues in the area to provide reconstructive and aesthetic surgical support for our veterans. I asked her if she had a medical director for the as-yet-unnamed nonprofit organization. She replied that she hadn't gotten that far yet. I volunteered immediately, and we got busy.

It quickly became obvious that our organization should be a national, not just a southern California program. I knew that many of my colleagues around the country who were busily doing face-lifts and breast surgeries like me would love the opportunity to show ourselves and the world that we were indeed *real surgeons.*

Reconstructive surgery, in which all of us had been well-trained, remained our link to more traditional medical care. It was what had

piqued my interest in plastic surgery in the first place. Even though
most of my professional life had been focused on aesthetic plastic
surgery, I was comfortable enough with trauma surgery to know
what I could do and what needed to be referred to specialists in allied
fields, such as hand surgery, eye surgery, dentistry or oral surgery, and
orthopedics or head-and-neck reconstruction. Besides, most of the
severe problems facing our veterans were being properly treated by
the VA, and those that "fell through the cracks" would be relatively
minor from a technical point of view—or so I thought.

Maggie decided to name the organization *Iraq Star*, pronounced
as in "Rock Star." The rhyming similarity was intentional. Maggie
felt that our honored wounded deserved to get first-class celebrity
treatment, perhaps to counteract the miserable reception our Vietnam
veterans endured. Our vets would be treated by America's best plastic
surgeons, whether in private practice or academia.

Within a few weeks, around two hundred members of the
American Society for Aesthetic Plastic Surgery in forty states had
signed on as volunteers. We were overwhelmed with the enthusiastic
response. Virtually no one who had been asked to serve had refused.
The hard part then began, which was, quite surprisingly, attracting
the patients. Somehow, we had to let the veterans know we were
available to them. This was a totally new and unexpected wrinkle.
In a sense, we had expected them to come to us. To quote *Field of
Dreams,* "If you build it, they will come."

Maggie took up the challenge fearlessly. She traveled to veterans'
organizations, did mailings to veterans' support groups, and met
with military hospital staffs. Most were helpful. Oddly enough, the
most negative reception came from the very source we thought would
have lauded our efforts: the VA system itself. Maggie traveled to
several VA hospitals to present our proposals, and was received with
scorn and patronizing smugness by some of the administrative staffs.
The prevailing response: "We take care of *all* of our veterans' needs,

so why do we need *you*?" It seemed that many in the VA hierarchy viewed our efforts as an attempt to show that they were not doing their jobs adequately. Fortunately, she was not easily deterred.

In the spring of 2008, Maggie and I went to Washington, D.C., and met with the amazing staff at Walter Reed Medical Center. In contrast to her VA experience, the idea of Iraq Star was warmly received. We were moved to tears by the enthusiasm of the veterans we met, eagerly working with their physical therapists to learn how to use their new prosthetic limbs. One double amputee was bouncing a basketball against a wall, the physical therapist crouched behind him to catch him if lost his balance. Others were scampering up a rock wall, and others still were being carefully stretched out to release spasms that those who have lost limbs are often afflicted with.

We met devoted volunteers who acted as "moms" to the hospitalized veterans far from home, and we got to know many of the veterans themselves, some of whom became Iraq Star patients. The doctors and the nurses, who often outranked the doctors, were particularly enthusiastic, intelligent, and devoted. There was no sense of business as usual. We were also amazed by the quality of the facilities in that venerable, older institution, and by the beauty of the campus on which it sits, a vast park area with spotlessly preserved older outbuildings designed to house outpatients and their families.

There had just been a spate of the worst kind of hatchet journalism by the media, and everyone at Reed was feeling the political pressure and embarrassment it had spawned. An off-campus motel had just been purchased by the facility, and it was being used temporarily for visiting families. It had not yet been remodeled, and televised scenes of mold in the bathrooms reflected terribly on the otherwise pristine condition of the rest of the vast medical complex. I had never realized the damaging and demoralizing power of an unchallenged media report. Everyone I had spoken to about our Walter Reed experience *absolutely knew* that the hospital was in ruinous condition. They were happy and surprised to hear otherwise.

We also met with the Undersecretary of Health for Veterans' Affairs, who received us politely, if condescendingly. I suppose that was not completely unexpected. Maggie and I were the most outside of Washington outsiders, and were probably seen in their minds as a couple of fancy Beverly Hills do-gooders. It was interesting that one of the assistants took us aside after the meeting, told us how much she appreciated what we were trying to do, and recommended a few other veterans support organizations that we could work with.

It was a start.

❖ *Patient Number One*

Although we thought at first that our work would involve relatively minor scars, our first patient, a young marine staff sergeant from Camp Pendleton quickly proved us wrong. He had been riding in an armored personnel carrier that had been destroyed by an IED, by far the most lethal weapon in the war and the most frequent source of severely wounded patients. He was lucky, because only the right side of his face had been destroyed. Others in the vehicle were killed instantly or died shortly afterward. When he woke up a few days later in the evacuation hospital in Germany, the first stages of repair had been done.

Further work was done after he returned to the states,involving many surgical proceures. When his wounds finished healing, his tongue was tightly scarred down to the floor of his mouth, making it nearly impossible to swallow food or to speak understandably. He fed himself a blended nutritional goop every few hours by means of a gastrostomy tube that went directly through his abdominal wall and into his stomach. To make matters worse, his wife was unable to deal with the trauma and stress of the situation and went home to her parents, leaving him in charge of raising their two-year-old son.

Paul's wounds were not minor by any means, and they required the services of a very specialized surgical team. We discovered that Iraq Star could also serve by facilitating referrals to appropriate specialists, and that has grown into a major part of our efforts.

Maggie searched for a physician known for expertise in reconstruction of the floor of the mouth and found Dr. Bruce Haughey in St. Louis. By means of some of the funds we had been able to raise, Paul was flown to St. Louis for evaluation. Iraq Star also received aid from Project Angel Flight, a nonprofit organization of retired commercial and private pilots who volunteered to fly our veterans and their families wherever they needed to be taken. Paul's father was flown to join him in St. Louis by their good graces.

Paul had his surgery in October of 2007—a twelve-hour procedure—then spent a week in the ICU with a tracheotomy, which enabled him to breathe until the swelling in his throat went down. He stayed another two weeks in the hospital before he was discharged. The hospital expenses were enormous, but because he was still considered active military, Tricare, the U.S. Armed Forces version of Medicare, paid those expenses. After his discharge, he went back to Camp Pendleton with his son.

His speech was improving, and he began to eat soft foods. Eventually the feeding tube was removed.

At the end of November, Maggie received a call from our U.S. Marine staff sergeant. His voice was much clearer and easily understood.

"Maggie," he said, "I had turkey for Thanksgiving."

❖ *A Question of Priorities*

Army Veteran Neil heard about Iraq Star from some of his army buddies. He sent an e-mail asking if Iraq Star could help with a scar on his face that bothered him. We asked him to send some photos so that I could make a referral to one of our volunteer surgeons in the Denver area, where he was living.

The photos came, and the first one showed a linear scar on his right cheek. It was the type of scar that could easily be dealt with by means of a garden-variety scar revision or perhaps with a Z-plasty, a tried-and-true means for breaking up a linear scar and realigning it so it becomes less noticeable.

The next photo showed a much more significant issue. It was a picture taken by a wire service that showed Neil jogging around the White House grounds with President Bush. He was wearing shorts, and he was springing along jauntily on his prosthetic legs. An IED blast in Afghanistan in December 2005 had taken his real ones.

Maggie called him and said, "Neil, you never told me that you lost your legs!"

"Maggie, that doesn't bother me. I've got that part knocked. It's this damn scar on my cheek that bugs me no end."

Neil was in Denver training for the Paralympics, and Dr. Rick Albin, one of our volunteers in that area, was all too happy to fix the scar.

❖ *Keep on Smilin'*

Tony had also been wounded by an IED, which was a particularly unlucky event for one in his type of duty. His job was to don protective gear and detect and disarm those devices before they killed someone. His arm had been broken in several places and hie jaw had been shattered. Once most of his wounds had healed, he had good mobility and strength, but the hard part for him was that he was missing many teeth and others were badly broken.

Here I reached out to a good friend and colleague in the Beverly Hills area, a superb cosmetic dentist. Dr. Larry Rifkin offered his services to Tony and restored a beautiful smile at his own expense without any fees. (I can vouch for his usual fees, being a patient of his myself. They are high, which, coming from me, means *high*.)

After Tony got better, he re-upped for another tour in Iraq. This is a common example of the bravery and dedication of our military. They want to rejoin their units and finish the job despite the risk to themselves.

Sad to say, he was once again wounded, this time more severely. He was back again on detail as a "Render Safe" warrior. On this particular occasion, the troops had detected the bomb and sent in the robot to eliminate the danger. Both the military and the Iraqi police thought it now a dud. About 7-8 men were around the IED for about an hour and a half when, without any warning, it detonated. Tony's very good friend was killed on the spot, and several others were seriously wounded.

A medic was in a truck nearby and although seriously injured himself, crawled over to Tony and saved his life. Tony's right wrist was shattered but salvageable, and his left leg was blown apart below the knee. After many operations and months of rehab he was able to walk again with a cane. Tony's concern upon admission to the hospital was that Maggie should be notified that his new teeth were still okay.

He most recently flashed his perfect smile while standing in his crisp Marine dress blues by the altar, watching his beautiful bride walk down the aisle toward him. A "halo" bone fixation device surrounded his lower leg through his neatly pressed white slacks. The medic was at Tony's side. He was all right.

I hope he finds another line of work once he's recovered.

❖ Saved By a Whisker

Staff Sergeant Jeff was wounded in Iraq on October 1, 2007. (Every one of these brave wounded warriors can tell you the exact date and time of their life-altering injury.) He was on patrol with his platoon in Anbar Province when the fins of a misdirected friendly-fire RPG sliced through left cheek and across his upper shoulders. As he fell forward, another RPG, this one from the enemy, struck the vehicle in front of him. The explosion shattered the bones of his left leg. It was only the immediate presence of the medics that saved Jeff's life; he was rapidly losing blood from three wounds.

After months of hospitalization and many operative procedures, his injuries healed. He regained his ability to walk after much physical therapy, but the cheek laceration had traumatized the facial nerve, leaving his mouth drooping to one side and an angry scar across his face that extended from the corner of his mouth to just behind his left earlobe.

Jeff was about to get married, and was despondent that he might never smile again. Iraq Star referred Jeff to one of our volunteer surgeons in Maryland, Dr. Brian Gastman. Dr. Gastman performed the corrective surgery in two stages. Jeff's nerve healed with time and he has his smile back and a rosy outlook on his future.

Jeff spent three years at Walter Reed Hospital both as inpatient and outpatient. Iraq Star was there for him for the last year of his recovery.

❖   *Keeping Spirits Up*

Iraq Star is growing daily, fulfilling a greater variety of needs. I recently examined a young woman soldier in my office, a retired army captain, whose injuries led to amputation of the left leg below the knee and left her with terribly deforming scars covering most of her thighs and buttocks. She also had lost the vision in her left eye. Her doggedly positive outlook led her to a career as a motivational speaker for fellow amputees. Making lemonade from lemons, indeed.

Her personal tragedy is that her deformity prevents her from dating, which under any other conditions would be easy. She is pretty, intelligent, and funny. More than anything, she wants to get married and have a child. Despite her ability to motivate other injured veterans, she cannot overcome her own fears of intimacy. She fears a horrified reaction to her scars should such a situation present itself. She's completely blocked before she can start.

Because she lives in Virginia, I referred her to a colleague who heads up the plastic surgery program at Georgetown. They will be starting work on her fairly soon. I expect any improvement, no matter how slight, will be very gratifying to her, and hopefully will give her enough confidence to recognize how attractive she really is.

As the war in Iraq appears to be winding down, the conflict in Afghanistan is heating up. Many more of our young servicemen and servicewomen will continue to struggle in far off lands, living in a constant state of danger. Some of these brave warriors will die, and many more will be wounded, returning home with deformities ranging from minor scars to severe mutilations. The need for reconstructive surgery will not end with the cessation of hostilities, whenever that may come.

Our volunteer surgeons can't completely erase the wounds of war, although that is our ultimate goal. The improvements we see with our veterans are the same that we see every day in aesthetic plastic surgery. Although most of them have suffered very serious injuries and have undergone many operations, it seems that it's often the most insignificant scars that are the biggest hindrance to their recovery. Repairing these works a kind of leverage; even the smallest improvement can yield a huge benefit in self-confidence. *And there's nothing more contagious or attractive than self-confidence.*

Iraq Star is one of several organizations that provide gratis reconstructive surgical help to our veterans. Occasionally, a bit of ego-driven competition arises between organizations. Surgeons are genetically determined to be competitive individuals. When this happens, we remind ourselves that we are all working for the same good cause, providing help to those who have risked everything in the service of the country. Good war or bad war, these are all brave young Americans, and we owe them whatever help we can give to make them whole again.

EPILOGUE
REFLECTIONS

Looking back, I see many changes that have occurred in my profession; some of them have elevated the specialty by providing better, more predictable and safer results with less invasive procedures. I've also seen a cheapening, a widespread commercialization of the specialty, with surgical outcomes that range from horrendous to others that defy any sense of normal human proportion. National chains offering inexpensive easy-in and easy-out face-lifts are proliferating. Billboards by the freeways offer breast augmentations at cut-rate prices. The dedication to quality of care is caving in to the pressure of the lowest standards of mass marketing.

Medicine in general has changed dramatically (and will no doubt continue to do so), and plastic surgery is not immune to those changes. The one-on-one personal contact between physician and patient has become severely eroded, and is in danger of slipping away completely. I'm extremely grateful for the opportunity to have practiced during a period in which doctors were seen as physicians, not *healthcare providers.*

I've also seen many changes in myself. I clearly have grown older: I have wrinkles on my face, an occasional aching back, and a bit less hair on my head than I once did (okay, more than a bit). I feel the same regrets that my patients feel when it becomes clear that the fun in the sun I experienced so many years ago has come back to haunt me. I, too, find myself holding my cheeks up with my fingers, pulling my neck taut, doing all the little maneuvers that my patients have done for so long.

But I haven't changed completely: I've managed to maintain my own sense of proportion and reality in an environment that promotes excess and unreality, for which I thank my Midwestern upbringing. That's not to say that I haven't dug the weather, the creativity, the excitement, and even the baloney of this strange Land of Oz ; I just haven't completely surrendered myself to it. Perhaps that's what allows me appreciate the Hollywood life and still relate to the inner core of humanity in the worldly, powerful and beautiful people who seek my services.

Is all my work but vanity? It's true that I haven't saved many lives since I completed my surgical residency. My work has improved people's lives in more subtle ways. Over the past thirty years, I have skirted the indistinct barrier between healthy and unhealthy narcissism in thousands of patients, with only a few missteps. I like to think that my work has contributed to their *healthy* sense of narcissism, to their self-confidence, to their self-esteem, and to their relations to their personal worlds.

For myself, I cannot imagine how I ever could have arrived at a better career choice. I have a knack for and enjoy fixing things. I love the creative improvisation that expertise in surgery or music permits, and I enjoy making people happy, especially women. It would appear that my life has unfolded exactly as it was meant to, beginning as a dream in my little nest under the dining room table, on a cold New Year's Day in Chicago.

I've moved to California, I've married a blonde, I've driven convertibles.

I watch the Rose Parade on television.

Some things never change.

ACKNOWLEDGMENTS

This little book has been in my head and in my laptop for almost ten years. That long, long time is due more to the fact that I have a busy day job than to its length or the amount of research I had to perform to write it. I looked no further than inside my own memory bank for the stories that I relate. The individuals I describe in these tales, although *incognito*, are those to whom I send my most sincere thanks. They and their stories have illuminated my own life.

I do have many identifiable people to thank as well. I never realized how talented my sister, Carol Bryant Story, could be as an editor. Whether acting alone or by channeling the brilliant intellect of our mutual high school English teacher, Dr. Margaret Annan, she mercilessly rejected my errors of syntax and excessive wordiness (she hasn't seen this last sentence, but it is what it is.)

To the editorial staff at iUniverse, who helped me with errors of punctuation and spelling—I will forgive them for questioning if *plotz* was a foreign language.

To my longtime surgical consultant Suzanne Rowins, for her completely undetached corroboration of these tales.

To my son Jeff Leaf for both suggesting the title and helping with the cover design.

To Micaela Bensko for shooting the cover photo and to Kelly for providing the goods.

To my colleagues at Leaf & Rusher Skincare—Rand Rusher, Curt Meeuwsen, and Harry Haralambus—for their encouragement and support.

To Maggie Lockridge, RN, and all the volunteer surgeons in the Iraq Star Foundation, for helping our brave veterans tell their stories. A portion of royalties from sales of this book will be donated to the Iraq Star Foundation. (www.iraqstar.org)

To my wife, Judy Brand Leaf, for her wit and humor, but not her patience; yes, Jude, the book is finally done. But I do like writing, so there may be more.

And to my dear family, friends, and colleagues who laughed at the funny parts and not the serious parts, my thanks.

NORMAN LEAF, MD, FACS

Born and raised in Chicago, Dr. Norman Leaf graduated from the University of Chicago School of Medicine with AOA Honors, and he later trained in surgery and plastic surgery at Stanford Medical Center and the University of Chicago Hospitals and Clinics. For more than thirty years, he has had a thriving private plastic surgery practice in Beverly Hills, California, and he currently serves as an associate clinical professor in the Division of Plastic Surgery at UCLA Medical School. In 1999, he created and opened the first freestanding salon for medical-grade skin care in Beverly Hills, and he is the co-creator of the Leaf and Rusher Skincare product line, featured at Saks Fifth Avenue in Beverly Hills and at high-end specialty stores and spas internationally.

He is the author of numerous scientific papers in surgical and plastic surgical journals, and he has appeared as a plastic surgery expert on many nationally broadcasted television shows, such as *The View, Woman to Woman*, and *Hour Magazine*, in addition to shows on the BBC and ITV in the United Kingdom. For many years, Leaf served as a consultant for motion picture and television productions as chairman of the AMA Physicians Advisory Panel for Motion Picture, Television, and Radio. He is currently the medical director of Iraq Star, a nonprofit organization dedicated to providing reconstructive and aesthetic plastic surgery services to injured U.S. veterans of the Iraq and Afghanistan wars.

He resides in Beverly Hills with his wife, Judy. He has three grown sons, one daughter, four grandchildren, and a dog named Cherry.

LaVergne, TN USA
29 April 2010
181064LV00004B/1/P